Charles Heathcote has  very rarely leaves. A MMU Cheshire and Creative Writing Grou[and prose. Our Doris is his first collection of monologues.

To Sarah

OUR DORIS

Charles Heathcote

Best Wishes

Charles Heathcote

VA
VARIOUS ALTITUDES
Cheshire

www.variousaltitudes.com

1

SLUGS

Our Doris has developed an unhealthy obsession with slugs. She's in the garden from Breakfast until The One Show finding the beggars and pouring salt on them. She likes to watch them die; keeps her eyes peeled as they shrink, curling in on themselves until they resemble ... well, dead slugs, really. I never was one for similes – a dead slug is a dead slug in my book and you can beggar off trying to tell me otherwise.

She did try using beer for a while, until I discovered where all of my Guinness were going. I wouldn't mind if our Doris had a drinking problem – she might be less keen to donate my socks to Sue Ryder – but I do mind when she's using my well-earned ale to pickle slugs.

You should see her on a morning. She'll come into the lounge with a cup of tea in one hand and a bucket of pellets in the other. I say to her, I say, 'What're you doing with that bucket, our Doris?'

And she gives me the Look, all squinted eyes and pursed lips. 'What do you think I'm doing, our 'arold, holding a flaming séance? I'm going to murder the beggars,' she says.

She's got a new smile, enjoys herself more than she ever did at the Co-Op. Not that she didn't have fun there – if someone let her loose with a pricing gun, she'd add twenty percent to the potted beef and reduce the whisky – she's always had a thing for Famous Grouse, says it reminds her of her mother. I say it'd be hard not to considering our Doris's mother drank that much grouse it were a wonder she could leave the house on the glorious twelfth.

Either way it got back to our Doris's manager and she were out on her ear. Someone had complained apparently; something about how their brother-in-law had spent his life savings on whisky, he was back three steps on his Alcoholics Anonymous program, and he currently inhabited her airing cupboard, which she wouldn't mind had she not just purchased several inexpensive items from Laura Ashley and he'd used them as hand towels when they were guest towels.

Not that our Doris minded. She always thought the Co-Op were beneath her – I remember when she first got the job, she were sixteen and full of exuberance, excitement and the wherewithal to throw Pink Ladies at any man whose hands found themselves creeping too close towards her Granny Smiths.

Then she found out that Janice Dooley of Little Street had found a job at Gadsden and Taylor as an office girl for Mr Gadsden himself. She became completely and utterly incensed. I were certain that our Doris were going to develop a twitch – of course we weren't together then, but as someone who frequented the Co-Op to observe a certain shop girl's Pink Ladies, I'm quite positive it were nothing short of a twitch.

Our Doris were like a woman possessed. Within the first week of her discovery, she had spread the rumour that Janice and Mr Gadsden were having at it in the storage cupboard. It didn't matter that Mr Gadsden were forty-seven and couldn't see his feet for his belly – it doesn't take much for folk to look at you differently. Everyone fancies spreading rumours about you; it takes away from the drudgery that is common life. I mean it was easy enough to imagine because it was difficult for Janice to rub two pennies together and most had it in their heads already that her father had bought her way in.

A fortnight later and pictures emerged in the Gazette of Janice and Mr Gadsden leaving the factory at the same time. Within the month Janice had been given leave from the factory to visit long lost relatives in Canberra, and Mr Gadsden had her job advertised in the post office window.

This coincided with our Doris's release from the Co-Op and she got the job. When Janice Dooley returned, she tried to spread the rumour that our Doris had spread lies, but no one could believe that of a shop girl who reduced whisky so as their grandparents could get rid of ailments from the common cold to laryngitis.

I know our Doris won't give up until she's committed slug genocide – until our back garden is awash with their corpses.

She came in this morning in what she calls her Felicity Kendal. I said to her, I said, 'What're you wearing that for, our Doris, you're going to get yourself filthy anyway.' The Look came with a side of hands on hips, pressing in the baggy sides of her dungarees. She said to me, she said, 'One must present themselves at their best at all times, our 'arold, if you haven't figured that out in fifty-four years I don't know what you've been doing. Besides, if those slugs know what's good for them, they'll know that the second I see a spot of mud on my blouse, I will boil them in a pot whilst their heart's still beating and take escargot to the next Bring and Buy.'

I think it's one too many repeats of The Good Life on Gold but I've kept my mouth shut, no point begging to be lambasted about why she had to spend twenty pounds on gloves when I had a perfectly good pair in the shed. She's hidden the price tags of her dungarees, so I'll thank the Lord for small mercies.

Three weeks ago, our Doris stormed into the front room, tore off her gloves finger by finger and threw them at my feet. She paced back and forth, back and forth across the bleeding carpet – almost pierced the floor with her high heels – and she doesn't just speak the information like any reasonable wife might do to her unsuspecting husband of half a century, no, she throws herself in both barrels yelling, bleeding heck she yelled, 'Can you believe it? I mean, can you believe it, our 'arold? The cheek of it. The bloody small-minded cheek of Violet bleeding Grey!' I were going to respond, but my lips had barely parted when she inhaled and her mouth kept on running, 'She knows I've wanted to be part of the garden safari for how long now, and this year she conveniently misplaces my entry. Misplaces, she says, she's never managed to misplace her bloody husband, even after he made advances towards Henrietta Wicks during the blackout of August 1972.' She burst towards the window and peered down the road, the tip of her nose pressed against the glass, eyes darting side to side. I felt sure she were going to tear down the curtains and use them as a noose.

I said to her, I said, 'So are you in the safari or not, our Doris?'

Her eyes stopped being part of her face at that point. She glared at me and said, she said, 'Oh, I'm part of the competition, our 'arold. Do you know what she said to me? She came over all glum, and she knows I can't say anything because she's sat between Mrs Cribbins and Mrs Patel and she knows all about how I'm planning on inviting them to my next garden party, and they sure as my name is Doris will not RSVP if they see me point the finger at Violet doe-eyed Grey.'

I lost my thread here. Only five minutes before, I'd been sat proudly reading the Daily Mirror, when in she came and blew my train of thought to smithereens. So I put my paper down and I said to her, I said, 'If you're part of the competition, what's the problem?'

'What's the problem? What's the problem? Do you want to know what the problem is, our 'arold? We're the first house! House number one. No one will pay any attention whatsoever to the flowers – they'll definitely not ask me about what compost I use.' I didn't have the heart to point out that I'm the one who gardens and she's the one who sits in the deck chair, sipping cups of tea from Whittards' best china cups. It wouldn't have mattered any which way because she kept harping on about her dress and how she'd seen just the one she wanted in Debenhams that screamed decorum with the added bonus of being high street, so she needn't worry about anyone thinking she thought she was above them and too hoity-toity.

And that's when she mentioned them. She said, 'And have you seen the garden, recently? It's practically riddled with slugs – slugs. Most people put down pellets, but no, what does my husband do? He bloody farms them. Tell me, our 'arold, did something I said convince you that the best recourse would be to fill my garden with gelatinous pests? Give me a swarm of locusts any day.'

After that I've had to bear three weeks of our Doris, the serial killer. If David Attenborough ever turned up in our garden wanting to film a feature on the common garden slug, the most he'd find would be an older lady picking up the inebriated beggars with a trowel and dropping them into a bucket.

She went one step further that morning. After presenting herself as Cheshire's answer to Felicity Kendal – looking more like a burnt sausage in denim – our Doris sat down in the chair beside me. Now our Doris only sits in this chair when she wants to talk to me, otherwise she is in the office writing letters, or in the high-backed Victorian armchair she spent five hundred pounds on because it gave off just the right air of class without being pretentious.

I knew it were important so I turned off the television. Something I don't do meekly, our cat once dug up her at Number 42's daffodils, and I didn't stop him until I saw Richard Hillman drive Gail into the canal.

Our Doris smiled, something else that doesn't happen often, and said to me, she said, 'Our 'arold.' She stretched it out so that it sounded something like a cat mid-miaow. 'You know you usually go down to the allotment on Wednesdays.'

I said to her, I said, 'Of course, I know, our Doris, 'it's the only day you'll let me go free.' If I had my choice I'd be down there from noon till night, but I get three days out of the week, Monday, Wednesday and Friday – all the days where our Doris is either otherwise engaged or wants me out from under her feet.

'Well,' she said to me, all fluttering eye-lashes and puckered lips, 'would you like to maybe take me? I'd love to see what you've done with the place, and besides,' she licked her lips at this one, she knew she had me, it's a move wives have perfected over the years, she said, 'I don't think we spend enough time together.'

I said to her, 'What do you mean, we don't spend enough time together, we bleeding live together.'

The damage had been done. Our Doris reigned supreme once again and I had to figure out how to break it to the lads. When I first got the allotment, our Doris came down to complete an inspection, didn't want her husband giving folk the impression that she didn't have enough for him to do at home. Then she discovered that Edith let Alf go down to get him out of her hair and if Edith Simpson's already doing it, our Doris needs to be at least two steps ahead.

Our Doris didn't make the best first impression, she put a deck chair in the middle of Fred's vegetable patch, which didn't go down well with the lads because his wife had just left him for an Audi saleswoman from Tunbridge Wells. She picked a prize marrow from Peter's plot and said she'd grown it herself. The allotment ended up declared a No Doris Zone.

Which is how I found myself at The Hare and Horse, drinking half a bitter shandy with Alf who'd already found his way through a pint and half. He were in a state of bliss, he'd had a win on the horses and managed to get out of Tesco without security noticing he'd made away with a six pack of Melton Mowbray and a bag of peanuts. His Edith wouldn't be happy, but usually he's disposed of the evidence by the time he gets home – says he goes to visit their grandson at the charity shop when in reality he's making off with the beggars from the old folk's home in the hope of a free meal and a lift home.

'So,' he said to me, armed with another pint, 'your Doris is ready to visit and you've not told her she isn't allowed?'

I put my wallet back in my pocket and nodded. I said to him, I said, 'I've never had the heart to tell her. We might not get on sometimes, but I'm not Genghis Khan.'

Alf laughed at this, mouth so wide you could see bits of pork pie on his tongue. He said, 'No, but your Doris will be when she finds out what you've been hiding.'

'Don't I know it,' I said, 'remember when your Edith had a new bathroom and I hadn't told her why you had to keep bobbing around ours for showers. I thought she were going to rip my face off and use it as toilet paper. Before I knew it we were at B&Q testing the finishes on bathtubs, and our Doris was using the cheque book that much the pages could've set alight and she wouldn't have noticed until the fireman were flinging her over his shoulder.'

'So· you want me to sweeten up the lads down the allotment?' Alf whistled between his teeth and rubbed his hands together. 'This is going to cost you something, 'arold, old chap – you think two pints is going to cover it? Oh no – I'll have to tell the big boss man and you know what that means, he won't settle for less than a sausage dinner with extra pickled onions.'

I said to him, I said, 'She's just one woman.'

Alf looked at me in a way I've only seen when he was slapped around the face by a trout and whistled again. 'She's never been just a woman, 'arold, she's

Doris.'

I couldn't sleep that night. I'd broken the news to our Doris that she'd have to wait until the Friday because they had a big project on, in actual fact I needed to give the lads time to acclimatise to the idea of Cheshire's very own Margaret Thatcher visiting their patch. Our Doris slept soundly, she'd had a good day in the garden and managed to slaughter seven slugs – I have a worry she'll leave them in her at Number 42's garden. It's not that she doesn't like her, it's just that she sees their garden as an unkempt display of everything that is wrong with British society.

She's not been happy since the council bought some of the houses on our street and let them out to people she deems part of the underclass she wants no part of. When her at Number 42 moved in, our Doris said, she said, 'Look at her – you should always give off the best first impression and what's my impression of her? She's too lazy to iron a blouse.' Things have got worse ever since – they nearly came to a head once, but our Doris refuses to reduce herself to such debauchery as parading insults in the middle of the street she has lived in her entire married life.

I'd have liked to have told her that it wasn't her at Number 42 who kept me awake at night, worried that my blood pressure would get that high I'd end up boiling to death. Sometimes I wonder whether I'd be better wearing a pulse monitor; I'd like to have some proper warning, rather than having to gauge our Doris's expression to see whether or not I'll end up dead by Granada Reports.

Another thing that kept me awake was the dulcet tones of our Doris's snoring. There's this certain quality to it that stops you from sleeping. Imagine yourself in

Africa – you're there trying to sleep at night when an elephant with a sinus infection decides to come and sneeze in your ear.

At breakfast the next morning, our Doris threw back her muesli whilst I found it difficult to get bread from the bread bin to the toaster. I had this silent hope that she'd forgotten all about the allotment – that it had been some whim, some rush of the menopause left dormant due to excessive use of HRT.

She sat there, spoon in one hand, copy of the Daily Mail in the other, reading all about how eating too much celery can lead to cancer. There's no issue for me there then, I've not been able to chew celery since I got my dentures, no matter the amount of Fixadent I put on them.

I approached the toaster all quiet like, hoping that for once it'd remain silent when I popped me bread in. No such luck. Our Doris's head flew up and she were glaring at me – I'd rather have taken my chances with the Devil himself. She said to me, she said, 'I'm going out today to buy my outfit for this Friday, our 'arold, how do you think I should play it?'

I said to her, I said, 'You could play it however you bleeding like, and the lads wouldn't notice – they're focused, our Doris, like to keep to the task at hand.'

'But they know I'm coming?' she said.

I thought my own eyes would pop out my head then. I said, 'Of course they know you're coming, you think I'd let you down the allotment without telling someone – that'd be like sending a juggernaut into a cul-de-sac, that would, our Doris.'

She didn't know what to say to that. It's one of the good things about being married to our Doris, she doesn't tend to notice much when she's got her mind on something – the nine months when she were pregnant were absolute bliss, I can tell you. I had free rein to do what I like, I could eat chips every day, I could ride my bicycle for more than work purposes. In the end I came off my bike on a country road in Rainow and ended up with a broken arm. Our Doris weren't too happy, the bike were her only chance at showing off that she cared about the environment.

My toast popped up and I set about buttering it. Our Doris had her beady eyes on me so I said to her, I said, 'What's so bad about being the first house, our Doris?'

Her shoulders bunched, her eyes pinched shut and she said to me, she said, 'There are ten gardens in total, our 'arold. The first four houses don't get noticed, folk speed through them certain they're not missing anything. If you're the fifth house, people pay attention. They realise they've gone too fast and now they're at the halfway point and all they've got at home is a washing up bowl full of dishes and a Catherine Cookson that isn't living up to much. For the last seven years Violet Grey has been house number five. I can have a number five garden, our 'arold, I didn't marry you for a number one garden.'

I said to her, 'What did you marry me for then?'

'It weren't your brains, I can tell you,' she said.

'Why not make a garden that good people have to stop?'

She said to me, 'I could have a naked Susan Boyle singing the aria from Tosca and people wouldn't notice until they were eating their Christmas shortbread.'

'It's June.'

'Exactly.'

'What are you going to do? Violet's already

allocated the gardens,' I said.

She pursed her lips at this, shoulders back, and said to me, she said, 'I have arranged for the committee to come and view the garden next week. I am making an appeal.'

I didn't know what to say so I had a bite of my toast. I don't know what you're supposed to say to your wife of half a century when she treats a garden safari as seriously as the parliamentary election.

As soon as I could, I made a break for it. For the second day in a row I met Alf at the Hare and Horse to discuss strategies for the royal visit. He looked a bit shifty when I got there, something I hadn't seen since that time he bought seventeen cans of Caribbean Sunset paint from Little Sid before finding out he couldn't flog them because they caused allergic reactions and left twelve goslings with breathing difficulties.

I said to him, I said, 'What've you done now, Alf?'

Well if he didn't look like someone had stolen his favourite yo-yo I don't know what he looked like. He said to me, he said, 'Edie were wondering where I'd been all afternoon, I told her, I said right to her face that I'd been down the allotment.'

'And?' I said.

'Now she wants to visit – she's working out the dates as we speak. Something about keeping an eye on the menfolk without snooping. She doesn't want your Doris to get ahead of her.'

'But everything went down well with the big boss?'

'Oh aye,' he said, 'when I said that it were for the garden safari he were more than happy to. He's only gone and got himself seventh house, hasn't he?'

I gulped then and said to him, I said, 'I best get the

pints in.'

He said, 'You only drink halves.'

I said, 'Wait until our Doris finds out the news – I need all the Dutch courage I can get.'

On the Friday, I thought my head were going to explode. Our Doris hadn't reacted well to the news that the big boss had been placed at house number seven when she'd been relegated to first. She said to me, she said, 'How could you let this happen, our 'arold? After everything I have told you. The seventh house is halfway between the fifth and the tenth house, after this house they start flagging. This is the least pretentious of all houses – I bet he's having it off with Violet, I wouldn't be surprised, she doesn't care where men have been as long as they have a pulse and full control of their own bladder.'

She didn't talk to me on Friday morning, except to ask me about her outfit. I think my jaw dropped – my dentures could have fallen out, and I wouldn't have noticed until I couldn't tell my gums from my tongue. Our Doris were wearing jeans. Jeans. When jeans first came to our town, she refused to wear them. She's opposed denim for that long when she bought dungarees I thought she were in the midst of a stroke, and yet there she stood in front of me, in jeans and a blouse that I call purple but our Doris dubbed lilac.

I said to her, I said, 'You look like a gardener, our Doris.'

She let me have a smile and we were in the car and on our way before I had chance to finish my brew.

It takes five minutes to get from our house to the allotment. I opened the door for our Doris and she rose from the Corsa, slow and Dracula-like. I said to her, 'What do you think, our Doris?'

She didn't reply. Instead, she headed straight for the gate and flung it open. I have never seen the men look so worried – a tank could have come through and crushed their plots and they couldn't have been more terrified. Ben caught her gaze almost immediately – I saw the smile plant itself on her lips, the one that says she's found her prey. You're just waiting for the fangs to come and tear out your jugular.

Without stopping to let me through the gate, she tore forward and planted herself in front of Ben's plot. They're not big, only enough space for a shed and a few rows of vegetables, but at that moment every man in the place looked like he wished there weren't so much space.

Ben's mouth didn't know what to do with itself. He made some circles, stammered some words, gulped before settling for, 'How do, Doris?'

Our Doris beamed and said to him, she said, 'Hello Ben, you do look well and how's Elaine?'

He wiped his brow, and took a breath that large I think he soaked up half the oxygen. 'She's all right, thanks,' he said – folk'll try that with our Doris, keep to the minimal reply hoping it'll move her along.

It didn't. She said, 'Good, and what're you doing with yourself today?' She glanced at this plot and unlatched the gate, stepping in. 'It appears you've been weeding – they're such pests aren't they?' With that she marched towards Ben's shed and grabbed a vat of Roundup and opened it up.

Ben rushed across, eyes wide, stammering, he said, 'Actually, Doris, I were planting – ' But it were too late. Our Doris rushed up and down the plot like a woman possessed – she hadn't been pouring long when Ben stopped her. His face were no more pink than beetroot.

He said to her, he said, 'What do you think you're doing? You come here – I know we were doing 'arold a favour by letting you come here, but pouring weedkiller all over a man's fresh seeds, it beggars belief.'

Our Doris's eyes flashed a Look in my direction. She nodded and placed a hand on Ben's arm. 'It's quite all right, you haven't, you haven't yet gained the expertise necessary to determine whether or not your plot needs a good pruning. Ask our 'arold if you can borrow his fork – I'm absolutely positive that he'll have something suitable in his workroom.' With that, our Doris left the plot and by way of farewell, added, 'Do tell Elaine I asked after her, it's been so long since last we met, that I am sure there are a great many topics to catch up on.'

As our Doris moved ahead, I made my way to Ben's plot. 'What's the damage?'

He looked at his freshly sown plot and shook his head. 'I don't know, 'arold, at least I stopped her before she did anything too bad. Why did she want to come down here anyway? Last I heard she'd given up on gardening in favour of the theatre.'

I said to him, I said, 'She did – but then that Violet Grey came up with the garden safari, didn't she? And haven't I known it every blithering year since.'

Before we could continue there were an almighty scream. I thought someone must have stepped on a cat's tail, there was a belated air raid, an ambulance had run over a whoopee cushion – I did not expect to see our Doris with her foot in the middle of Peter's prize marrow.

Only Peter weren't screaming – I wasn't even sure he was living. He'd collapsed on the ground, the colour drained completely from his face.

No, it were our Doris, wailing like a banshee.

''arold,' she screamed, 'look what this great blithering vegetable has done to my new plimsolls.' She pulled her leg free so that I could see her leg covered in a green gunk. She caught sight of Peter and I've never seen her fly into more of a rage. 'And then the beggar thinks it's the best time to bloody sleep – never in my life have I seen such laziness. His father fought for this country and he thinks he can get away with ruining my M&S plimsolls by lying down amongst the vegetables. I will send him my dry cleaning bill. I will inform his wife.'

After checking Peter hadn't had some form of cardiac arrest, I took our Doris home.

Our Doris didn't find any new ways to commit slug slaughter. She strengthened her efforts to pour salt on them. If you'd gone into the garden that week you'd have been sure that we'd let it out to an alcoholic with a waste disposal problem. I'd only have to walk down to my shed to find half-cut slugs dwindling to an untimely death.

She stopped eating her meals and using antibacterial gel every time she touched a trowel. Her hair became matted, she didn't put on make-up. From dawn till dusk, our Doris lingered in the garden, ridding it of pests, planting flowers and hiding unsightly mounds of dirt with pebbles from Focus.

When she were finished she showed it to me and said, she said, 'What do you think, our 'arold?'

I said, 'It's fantastic, our Doris.' And I weren't lying – the garden were colourful, it looked as though someone had taken a small patch of land and replaced it with an art installation. It made me want to use similes – there were small delicate flowers and large blooming ones. Purples and pinks and blues and yellows and reds. The garden were the perfect embodiment of our Doris.

I said to her, I said, 'You'll be the fifth house before you know it.'

I should have kept my mouth shut, wish I'd kept my bleeding mouth shut, because what went and happened that night? A storm. In the middle of June – as though the forces of nature thought they could come along and put our Doris's work to shame.

Violet showed up in the morning with the committee. She's one of those women who hold their noses that high you're surprised they don't tip over backwards. She said to our Doris, she said, 'Good morning, Doris, such terrible weather we had last night, I hope that your garden was saved.'

Our Doris bit her tongue and said, she said, 'Oh, well you see Violet, there was a slight issue – the wind's torn my flowers to shreds and the stems have broken, the stones have all sunk in mud but there's still an abundance of something I'm sure you'll find familiar – you're both so alike after all.' Our Doris showed Violet to the garden, her head held high. She flung open the door, a grin on her face and said to her, she said, 'Slugs! Now, you mustn't be downhearted, Violet, I've always found you both to be delightfully slimy.'

2

LADiES DAY

Our Doris is an utter nuisance when it comes to going anywhere. Take last Thursday for example, I told her, I said, 'Hurry up, our Doris we have to be at the pavilion by half past.' My cousin was having a bash at bowls and I wanted to be there in case his knee went and he ended up cock-eyed on the floor with his nose impaled on a jack.

Do you know what she did? She said to me, she said, 'I need a new hat, our 'arold, this one won't do.'

I took one look at it and said, 'No, it won't.' It were bright blue with plastic gems stuck to it, I thought that's just my luck that is – a wife whose head resembles a peacock's backside. I didn't say this to her, though. No, I wasn't after a beating. I took my coat off the hook and said, 'Come on then.'

We went to town. Twenty minutes later I was stood in the centre of a charity shop whilst our Doris gave a volunteer the what for. She was all looked up, pierced eyes, pursed lips, face the colour of beetroot and she says, ''Ow can you charge these rates – they're bleeding extortionate. If I'd wanted to pay this much money I'd have gone to Harrods.' She'd never have gone to Harrods – she says it's too poncey, but I didn't mention this to her. By this time she'd attracted quite the scene. And then in all seriousness the volunteer took the hat and said, 'I'm sorry, but we try to do our best by our customers who are donating these items. All the money raised goes towards a good cause.'

I've never seen our Doris that mad, and that includes the time I hoovered up the hamster. She shouted, 'A good cause? I've scraped more of a good cause off my shoes. Come on 'arold.' I chased after her. She stayed quiet until we got to the car and she said, 'It's a good job I Silvakrinned my hair.' And we sped off.

She's always been the same – I think she only showed up for our wedding on time because she wanted to vet the guests before they went into the church.

Once again she caught me out of the blue – sprung it on me, she did. She's doing what she calls "damage limitation" – she were sat at the dining room table when she told me – we don't even have a dining room, it's a cubbyhole between the lounge and the kitchen. For her dinner parties we use the lounge but our Doris says that any self-respecting person of her social calibre should never be seen as not being able to afford a separate dining room for when she entertains.

Our Doris were currently writing her correspondence with the local news reporter at the Partridge Mews Gazette because she disagrees with the writer's views on spring rolls as a starter. It didn't stop her from stopping mid-prawn cracker and saying to me, 'I'm arranging a luncheon for the ladies group with pink champagne and seasonal aperitifs.'

I said, 'Oh.'

I let her stew and went back to scouring the stove. I'd had a mishap with a coq au vin the night before. I don't know why I bother, give me a steak and kidney pie any day, but our Doris is trying to make me more cultured. Besides, I get rewarded. I cook some foreign muck and she lets me watch Charlie Dimmock digging a trench – the way she handles a trowel is enough to make grown men weak at the knees.

'Well?' Our Doris said, her face a shade of puce at her husband's lack of gentlemanly conversational skills.

I said to her, I said, 'Well what?' I kept my eyes on the stove – if our Doris caught me with a smile on my face – or worse a grin – she'd use her letter writing skills to dislodge my retinas.

'Well, aren't you going to ask me why I'm holding a luncheon for the ladies group? There'll be pink champagne.'

I said to her, I said, 'I thought you said as you wouldn't be caught dead serving pink champagne in respectable society.'

This earned me The Look – she held up a finger and said to me, she said, 'One, this is not respectable society, they barely class as polite and two, I offended Violet Grey and have since been ostracized by the ladies for my thoughtless behaviour when Violet had been so kind as to offer me first house for the garden safari.'

I dropped my scourer then and slurped my tea. 'I thought being first house was a bad thing – folk wouldn't notice you,' I said.

She capped her pen then. I thought things must be serious if she's capping her pen. She bought it especially for official Doris correspondence – a fountain pen that cost more than a bottle of Glenfiddich and a box of Marlboro Lights. Not that I get the opportunity anymore – you get one bout of pneumonia and your wife's swapping your cigarettes for herbal tablets because she won't have Nicorette in her house, thank you very much.

Our Doris set her hands on the table and said to me, she said, 'Being awarded first house is the worst affront that can be committed. However, Violet Grey and I are the only two in that vile ladies group to pay enough attention to know these things.' Her pose reminded me something of Margaret Thatcher – a woman disliked by Doris, not for her politics, but for her shoulder pads. Our Doris is a staunch believer that no woman should have to dress like a man in order to be treated like a human being.

She said to me, she said, 'This luncheon is damage limitation. Pink champagne states that I am not worthy of Violet Grey, whilst the luncheon exposes a frank and heartfelt apology to the ladies group. Next year we will be fifth house and Violet Grey will have no choice but to smile and congratulate me on my splendid floral display.'

'Can't she still reject your display?' I said.

Her eyes sunk into her head, and her lips twisted into something resembling a smirk and she said to me, she said, 'I have a plan, our 'arold, and it involves something Violet Grey would be reckless to refuse.'

She went back to writing her letter and said no more about it.

I, meanwhile, ended up down at the Hare and Horse with Alf. He rang from the hospital, he'd been caught trying to smuggle four bags of M&Ms into the cinema. When the usher confronted him, he opened a bag and tried to down it – he ended up choking and within the next half hour he were in A&E, after an attempt to perform the Heimlich Manoeuvre on himself went wrong.

He said as it was too early to go home to his Edith, and besides, if our Doris were organising a luncheon I didn't want to be anywhere near the house with my car. Last time she arranged a dinner party, she decided that she needed to go down to Lincolnshire to find just the right kind of pork to display her impeccable taste. A normal husband might have balked at the idea, but a normal husband doesn't have our Doris for a wife. A few birthdays back, I bought her scent from a pharmacy rather than an actual perfumery. It were on offer, but there's nothing our Doris dislikes more than bargains, says that it displays utter thoughtlessness of the person that has helped to create such delicacies as Estee Lauder Youth Dew.

I got my sight back eventually – and I can now quite honestly tell folk about the cons of using scent to polish your irises.

She sent the Youth Dew to her cousin in Pontefract – they've not been on good terms since said cousin married an unemployed butler from Halifax. It's not that she disagrees with the idea of butlers, she'd love nothing more than to have someone properly shine her cutlery – no, it's the idea that her cousin would marry someone of such social standing.

Not wanting to end up having to drive our Doris across the country in search of the nation's finest crab cakes, I picked up Alf and headed straight for the pub. Alf set to ordering his usual pint and pork scratchings and I settled myself in for an afternoon of half a bitter and a packet of dry-roasted peanuts.

I said to him, I said, 'Why'd you empty your pockets, Alf?'

He gives me his grin then, all hunched shoulders and eyes peeking from side-to-side. 'It's Edith, she's decided she wants me to uphold impeccable behaviour wherever I go. The usher said to empty my pockets and I did, straight down the hatch.' He downed his lager and belched, giggling to himself. 'She'll soon give up this idea of having a husband who's something he's never been.'

'You're a braver man than me, Alf,' I said.

'No, I'm not married to Doris.' Alf gulped.

I said, 'You can't say fairer than that. She's organising a luncheon.'

Alf shook his head at that and threw back a few pork scratchings. ''arold, you poor beggar.'

When I got home I found our Doris buried behind three phone books. She said as she'd been looking all day for a butcher who could provide the right kind of chipolata – and that butchers were not the kind of person she ever wishes to enter into conversation with under any circumstances. I made her a brew and asked her what had happened. She said to me, she said, 'I rang to ask about the size of his sausage, and woe betide me believing that that sort of pre-pubescent penis humour went out with short trousers and potted beef sandwiches.'

'I rang seven different butchers across the county and each of them spent five minutes sniggering before delivering measurements that can only be described as woefully pitiful in length and girth, and is it too much to ask that chipolatas for a ladies luncheon be delivered skinless with more meat than gristle?'

I had to hide my smirk behind my hands. Our Doris has always had a way with innuendo – she nearly ended up in court once after a few choice words insinuated that the vicar had been having an affair with the post-mistress. And as she told them, if they'd been having an affair she'd have only used that information if it proved fruitful for her – she's not a gossip after all, merely an observer of the human psyche. She got that line from watching a few too many episodes of Miss Marple on ITV3.

I said to her, I said, 'Have you tried going straight to the farmer, our Doris? What would the ladies group say if they found out that the food was locally sourced?'

Well if our Doris's eyes didn't light up I'd swear that she had cataracts. 'That there, our 'arold is a brilliant idea. That would further emphasise the point that I care about helping local businesses whilst also highlighting my rapport with those not of my social standing.' She flicked through the Thomson Local at a pace Penelope Pitstop would be proud of. There were a grin plastered on her face I hadn't seen since that time she found out she'd won first prize for her jam at the summer fête.

I left her to it and went to turn on the telly. Ground Force weren't on so there went my hope of catching sight of Charlie Dimmock fondling an aspidistra. I found some quiz show and let it drown out the sound of our Doris heckling a farmer down the phone for his awful dirty mind and that as someone in such a profession he should not be making jokes.

The next morning she was up and poaching eggs before I had chance to fetch the newspaper. Our Doris has always had a thing about The Daily Mail – she reads the news and I take the crossword. It works two ways, the first being that our Doris tells folk I'm cultured enough to only do The Daily Mail crossword and the second being that our Doris leaves me be if I have a crossword in my hand.

I said to her, I said, 'How do you do it, our Doris? You didn't go to bed till three.'

She tapped her nose and set about putting bread in the toaster. She said to me, she said, 'A lady must never let her husband know her secrets.' I used this to gauge the situation – usually she'd tell me to keep my nose out of her business. Our Doris doesn't see kindness as the epitome of a relationship between a married couple – I brought it up on our tenth anniversary, I said to her, I said, 'Don't you think we should say that we love each other more?'

She gave me what I'd very soon identify as The Look and said, ''arold, if I'd wanted relationship advice when I married you, I'd have written into Woman's Weekly. I know that I'm married to you, you know that you're married to me – what more could you ask for?' Forty-four years later and she's still under the same opinion. She once got a bit squiffy at a Christmas do and told me she didn't marry me for my looks, but someone gave her a glass of water and soon put her right.

I sat down at the table and set about separating the news from the puzzles. It wasn't the first time our Doris had been as unnaturally kind as to make breakfast, last time had been when she wanted me to drive down to Lincolnshire for pork.

I was trapped.

Poached eggs on toast with the right amount of salt and pepper. A cup of tea with proper sugar because our Doris doesn't believe in aspartame. The fact that she'd made breakfast should have set alarm bells ringing.

There I was, at the kitchen table, my eyes on three across as I tried to think of the various ways I could wrangle my way out of this one, when our Doris reached across the table and tilted the paper away from my face with a teaspoon. ''arold,' she said, 'I've got something to ask you.'

I thought to myself, I thought this is it. This is the moment when you tell Doris, 'no'. It's been fifty-four years, there must be something in her head that allows just one negative answer. I remembered the Easter of nineteen-eighty-seven when she'd asked me to take her down to her mother's because her sister was over with the kids, but I was holed up in bed with flu. She responded well to that – she only hid the paracetamol until I started throwing up near her oak nightstand.

'I need you to drive me to Astbury. There's a farm there that might just have the type of chipolata I'm after for my luncheon.'

I breathed that heavy I'm surprised there was anything left in my lungs. Astbury. I could do that – eight miles down the road – take our Doris out for lunch and I'd be sorted.

Our Doris must have noted the smile on my face, she said to me, she said, 'That had better be a yes on your face, our 'arold, because you know how I feel about any of those unnatural urges of yours.'

'I'll take you to the farm, just let me finish my breakfast.'

I thought I'd got off easy. She said to me, she said, 'Good, because after that we need to go to Chester to check on how that city actually operates because Violet Grey has deemed it the city she goes to for all her exclusive shopping requirements. She left one of her bags out at the last WI meeting and I borrowed one of her receipts.' I think our Doris actually flourished as she took the receipt from the pocket of her pinny and spread it out on the table. 'This is the type of cheese she used in her cheese swirls – I wouldn't be caught dead serving something that fell out of fashion in the nineteen-seventies, but you know how Violet behaves.'

I said, 'You want to go to Chester to buy cheese?'

I earned half a Look then and she put the receipt back in her pocket. She said to me, she said, ''arold, I don't think you understand. This isn't just about apologising to Violet and regaining my rightful standing in the ladies group, this is about being the fifth house, this is about making Violet pay.' I swear our Doris could have been a mob boss in a previous life. If her and the Godfather had gone at it, I'm sure that Don Corleone would have ended up sleeping with the fishes sooner rather than later.

I sighed and smeared some yolk onto my toast. 'All right, we'll go into Chester – but all you seem to talk about are starters. When is this luncheon?'

She nibbled the edge of her toast and said to me, she said, 'Next Tuesday.'

'Tuesday? Tuesday?' I said, forkful halfway to my mouth. 'That's five days away. How do you plan on creating a luncheon in five days, our Doris?'

'I once single-handedly directed a full performance of The Sound of Music with the Partridge Mews Choral Society and Theatre Association, after only two week's rehearsal and a severe battle with a gastrointestinal virus that left me incapacitated throughout three run-throughs of My Favourite Things; I know something about creating splendour at short notice.'

I gulped and ate the rest of my breakfast in silence. She were a woman on a mission, and I am nothing if not a coward when it comes to my wife.

The farm smelt how farms smell – like manure. Cows mooed and swished their tails and altogether looked utterly gormless. The farmer came over and shook my hand. I've never seen a man's face disassemble into shock as fast as when he looked at our Doris. His mouth fell open, his eyes went wide.

I couldn't blame him, our Doris had chosen to wear what she deemed the appropriate attire for an agricultural conference. Yes, she had wellingtons, and yes she'd brought an anorak. It was the tweed skirt suit she'd bought from a specialist shop for lady farmers – those who have a man to come in and do all the work whilst they ride horses and have affairs in stables. A regular Kim Tate, minus the killing her husband part.

At least I hope she's never thought about killing me.

Our Doris took the farmer's hand and smiled that smile, the one where she looks as though she could rip a man's head off in an instant. 'Mr Harris?' she said, acting the Queen with a bob of her head. She said to him, she said, 'We spoke on the telephone concerning the length and girth of your chipolata.'

He hid a snort behind a cough and said to her, he said, 'Your Mrs –'

'This is my husband, yes, however his palate is not educated enough to appreciate the true splendour of a properly seasoned, artisan sausage.'

I shrugged my shoulders when he looked at me and said to him, I said, 'I'm more of a Richmond man, myself.' And I am, I can't go in for all this specialist sausage nonsense – especially when I could go out, purchase, fatten and butcher a pig for less myself. It'd only have to take one look at our Doris and it'd probably make sure its meat was perfectly marbled.

The farmer led us into a cottage. Our Doris covered her face with a hankie, not used to seeing muddy footprints all over the floor. A collie flew across the kitchen and jumped up at Doris, caking her tweed skirt in a layer of mud so that she ended up matching the tiles. She looked as though she would make sausages out of the dog then, rip open his guts and use his intestines as a skipping rope; I've never seen The Look so fierce.

'Down Cap!' Mr Harris yelled – he took the dog by the scruff of his neck and dragged him into the hall, slamming the door shut. He looked back at our Doris, the smile falling from his face. 'Sorry about that, Mrs Copeland.'

'Please just bring the sausages,' she said to him.

Mr Harris revealed his grill pan and our Doris revealed the Look – the full blown Look – so much of a Look a torpedo could have blown up half of the barn and Mr Harris would have looked less fearful of his future. She pursed her lips and said to him, she said, 'And you wonder why farming is a failing trade? I could go to Morrisons, or some other high-class brand of supermarket disassociated with the farming community – where I would not have to contend with the disgusting amount of filth this farm holds. I need not fear about being pounced on by a hound who looks more like a frayed pan scourer than an animal fit for rounding up sheep. I need not worry about salmonella or whatever other diseases are lurking in this –' she snorted here, actually snorted, as though flames were going to come bursting from her nostrils and she said, 'well I'm sorry but you can't call it a kitchen, it looks like it should have been condemned in the summer of nineteen-seventy-three. And then you reveal a grill pan that thick with fat I think half of it must have been squeezed from the overflowing droplets of Kerry Katona's last bout of liposuction.'

Mr Harris's hands were actually trembling – he set the grill pan back down and said to her, he said, 'Will you be taking the sausages then?'

'No, I will not be taking the sausages, I wouldn't take the sausages if they were made from apple-fed boars from bleeding Acapulco! This is a travesty. All I wanted was an artisan sausage for the starter at my luncheon for the ladies group; I will not serve them e-coli on a cocktail stick.' Our Doris didn't even stop to let me hold the door, she were sat in the front seat before I had chance to get the keys from my pocket.

We didn't get to Chester. Our Doris had me take her home so as she could disinfect her hands because it, 'isn't long since the last swine flu outbreak and I'm rather confident I just found the breeding ground'. She bathed for three hours, used up a bottle of Radox, and slept through two episodes of Emmerdale and a re-run of Poirot. When she came out of the bath, I wasn't sure whether the wrinkles were hers, or my wife had just turned into a prune.

A few days later and our Doris set out to her ladies group luncheon. She'd been to the florist and had actual carnations pinned to the top of her hat because she would be damned if she went around wearing plastic pound shop knock-offs. I didn't ask her about the price of her new suit, that she emphasised was peach not mushroom as some would call it.

She disappeared for six hours and I got to watch

an omnibus edition of Ground Force. I tell you, it's a good job I don't have a heart condition, the sight of Charlie Dimmock in those Levi's would have caused any man's pacemaker to go haywire.

Three quarters into the final episode, the front door slammed with such force the windows shook. It wasn't an intruder, not some ghost from the past wanting me to pay for my sins. No. I've heard that slam enough times in the last fifty years to know who it was and what it meant. Our Doris was home, and she was furious.

She roared into the front room and slammed her bag onto the floor, tearing her hat off her head and she positively howled, 'If I ever see Violet Grey again it will be a day too soon. The cheek of it! Can you believe it? I mean, can you believe the sheer impudence?'

I switched off Charlie Dimmock and faced my doting wife. 'What did she do, our Doris?'

She said to me, she said, 'I stood there, after the dessert, profiteroles with chocolate sauce – nothing too middle class, these women still believe that a Come Dine with Me cake with melted chocolate in the centre is the best thing since Victoria Sponge – and I issued my apology, "Please, Violet, accept my humblest apology for my callous attitude towards you upon your admission to my home. There is no excuse for such barbaric behaviour, although I hope you can find it in your heart to forgive me, bearing in mind that I had just found my garden destroyed by an act of our lord." And do you know what she did? She accepted my apology.'

I said to her, I said, 'I thought that's what you wanted.'

'Oh I wanted forgiveness, our 'arold.' She almost ripped up her hat at this point, the carnations were all but crushed. 'She forgave me. It's the next bit that makes me want to write a letter to the Gazette informing them of the fact that Mrs Violet Grey of Hobson Street has to use depilatory cream on her upper lip because she grows a beard the likes of which Father bleedin' Christmas would be proud of!'

'What did she do, our Doris?'

'What did she do? What did she do? I said to her, I said, "I would like to think we could reconcile this sorry mess by my entering into the garden safari again next year, so as we can properly put this to bed." Do you know what she did? Miss Fake Tears and No Knickers? She held a handkerchief to her face – Waitrose not Laura Ashley – and she said to me, she said in full view of the ladies group, mind you, "I would love nothing more than to accept your entry into the garden safari. However, I have an announcement of my own. Next year, I would like to focus more on my family. I will still chair the ladies group, but I have given leadership of the garden safari project to someone who can fully dedicate her time to making the safari a world class event." I thought I'd won, our 'arold.'

'Well?' I said.

'Well, well? What do you mean well?'

'Who's the new leader?'

'Who do you think, our 'arold? Who has been my mortal enemy since first year when she got the part of Mary in the Nativity and I got bleedin' narrator? Janice Dooley of Little Street.'

3

SCHOOL REUNION

Our Doris is organising a school reunion, I've no idea why since half of our classmates are dead and the other half have been written off as too close to the underclasses to correctly employ the proper decorum necessary for a themed dinner party. But that's our Doris for you, she once invited the Big Issue man to afternoon tea because she wanted to show off to Violet Grey that she cared about those in difficult circumstances. Once he left she had the upholstery steam cleaned and the couch disinfected.

It's all to do with this bleeding garden safari. Our Doris thinks that if she can get Janice Dooley of Little Street in the same room then she can convince her that our house is best suited to fifth house. I tell you I'd rather throw myself to a pack of rabid hyenas than spend one more night talking about shrubs and whether I could possibly move my shed to a more discreet location – somewhere no one would associate it with our Doris, I said to her, I said, 'Why don't I just camouflage it, our Doris, and save you the bother?'

She said, 'Would you?' And to cut a long story short I spent the best part of Saturday putting floral cellophane all over my shed – our Doris weren't happy either way because I'd used Poundstretcher dustbin covers. She said to me, she said, 'What've you done that for, our 'arold – they're nothing short of working class – imagine what Marcia at Number 47 will say. She'd be on the telephone to Pandra straight away to say as I have made another social faux pas.'

I said to her, I said, 'I suppose I should have found a long lost Lowry?'

She gave me the Look and said, 'You make me out to be some sort of harridan, our 'arold, though a long lost Lowry might appeal to some, I am a humble housewife who would be quite pleased with an eclectic fabric from Laura Ashley.'

I said I were going to the Hare and Horse and she rang her cousin in Mobberly.

After my second half I'd calmed down slightly – not much mind you, I'd still sooner pave over the garden and bury our Doris beneath the conservatory but we were getting somewhere. Alf showed up about six – he were on the run from the coppers, something about a misunderstanding with the manager of a Bargain Booze to do with misplacing three bottles of brown ale up his sleeves and down his trousers – he said as it weren't his fault he'd lost weight but the manager weren't buying it.

I bought him a pint anyway. He could tell something was up. His Edith said as if I were to support his alcohol habit much longer she would tell our Doris about my reading the Daily Mirror. I tell you, the women in this town are like the bloody SS. If Hitler had our Doris I'd be eating Bratwurst right now.

Alf said to me, he said, 'What's she done now?'

Well if I didn't go up like a bottle of pop I don't know what I did. 'She's planning a school reunion to get back in touch with Janice Dooley – had me bending over backwards. I've been to Crewe to Chester to Manchester – she'll have me going to outer bleeding Mongolia next, all so she can get on this garden safari. I wouldn't mind if she did any of the work but she can't tell the difference between hyacinth and hibiscus can that woman. I should've listened to my mother.'

'If you'd listened to your mother you'd be a monk – and no man's built for celibacy.'

'No man's built for our Doris, I can tell thee.'

I don't remember getting home but I did wake up in a wheelbarrow, soaked to the skin, our Doris standing over me with an empty mop bucket in her hand, 'Harold, if you would ever so kindly wake up, the neighbours are quite worried.' And with that our Doris scuttled off into the kitchen – some part of me wished it could've been that easy, that our Doris hadn't realised I were drunk and had thrown the bucket of water to make sure I weren't dead – when you've been married for as long as I have you get to know your wife, and when your wife happens to be Doris you question whether you'd have better chance hiding from the Gestapo.

Our Doris went into the kitchen and got out the Pyrex dish; it's always bad when she decides to make a casserole. When Mrs Dunlop of Forge's Row refused to let her star as Maria in the Sound of Music – said as she were too old and would she like the part of a nun? – the house were jam-packed with every sort of casserole from lamb to butternut squash. She gave the postman three because he delivered the gas bill on time.

I staggered out of my wheelbarrow and into the kitchen – once you get older you don't so much as get a hangover as wonder whether you've reached the end. I dosed up on paracetamol, statins and a few more drugs to keep me older for longer and looked at our Doris.

Before I'd opened my mouth she said to me. I say she said, it were reminiscent of a growl, if you've ever wondered what a dragon sounds like I'm sure you'd come close if you heard our Doris hissing at me. She said to me, she said, 'We have been married for half a century, our 'arold and I have never been more embarrassed than this morning. I thought maybe you'd done the considerate thing and had a heart attack, but no, who should I receive a telephone call from but Janice Dooley herself – can you tell me what she were doing walking past my place of residence at six o'clock this morning?' Our Doris raised her eye-brows at this, like an old headmaster, I wouldn't have minded if she'd beaten me – I've spent fifty years trying to develop a fetish but once you hit seventy-four I suppose all that goes out the window like being able to get a full night's sleep without the threat of wetting yourself. I looked down at myself, but the only damp patches had been flung from our Doris's mop bucket.

I looked her in the eye and I said to her, I said, 'Do you think I'd have an affair, our Doris? I tell thee it's enough being married to you, I don't have time enough in the world for Janice Dooley of Little Street.'

'I should think not,' she said, 'not when you're supposed to be helping me get fifth house.'

I don't know why I said what I said next. I think maybe it were the drink talking – either that or dementia. I think if you can't claim senility when you've been old for as long as I have then there's something wrong with the world. I said to her – and lord have mercy on my soul – I said to her, I said, 'I've had enough of your garden safari, our Doris.'

She didn't give me the Look. I could have coped with the Look – after fifty-four years of marriage you get used to your wife having eyes like nuclear missiles. No, what she did next, well I'd never have thought it of our Doris – she once argued with a toddler when he cut the line at the Co-Op – our Doris put down the casserole dish and left the house. She took her floral print Cath Kidston bag and Laura Ashley coat 'that was not dissimilar yet made for quite a startling contrast' and left the house.

I didn't think much of it. She might have thought I'd follow her, but I were soaked through to my skin, hungover and in need of a bacon sandwich – our Doris had had fifty years of my time, I'd be glad to have a few hours alone.

I did what any man would have done in my situation. I stayed home.

I have learnt in my lifetime that it is best not to follow our Doris unless you are well dressed and your manner is impeccable and you happen to be royalty. Otherwise she is liable to ignore you until she finds a policeman at which point she will claim that you have been harassing her and have you spend the remainder of the day behind bars. This is how I spent our thirtieth anniversary. Our Doris had her eyes set on this new restaurant in the middle of town – they had the kind of serviettes that weren't made of paper and low lighting and the mayor had opened the place; a proper certified do that she wasn't invited to. I said to her, I said, 'What do you want to go there for anyway, our Doris? You're short sighted enough as it is without lights so dim you'd think there'd been a power cut.' She'd insisted. She said to me, she said, 'Janice Dooley has already been seen in a booth with Mr Todd and his divorce has only just come through. You'll be able to get a reservation, our 'arold, I am a reputable member of the ladies group.' I must have tried for days to get a reservation, ringing every few hours to see if someone had cancelled, popping in when I had a few minutes off work.

Then I got the phone call.

A cancellation – someone's birthday party wouldn't be happening because they'd broken their ankle on a helter-skelter in Grimsby.

I told our Doris I'd got a reservation. She bought herself a new dress from one of those boutique shops and had her hair done, she looked a dream. We parked in front of the restaurant. She'd given her coat to a maître d', were scouting the place like a lioness after a gazelle ... and they had no reservation for us. Her eyes glazed over, her lips pursed, she gripped her purse with all the rage of a scorpion under a boot, and she stormed over to the diary.

And she found the name.

The name set for the next day.

I said to her, I said, 'I must've got my dates mixed up, our Doris, we'll come back tomorrow.'

She got her coat and walked away.

I might have spent the night in a cell for stalking a middle-aged woman but it were the best night's sleep I'd had in the last thirty years, I can tell you. If our Doris isn't snoring she's regaling me with tales about Violet Grey and her arthritic hip.

If I'm honest, I didn't mind her leaving me in the house on my own; you can't watch an episode of The Royal with our Doris going on about how she could have been an actress if her career at Gadsden and Taylor hadn't taken off – she had one line as Second Shopkeeper in the Partridge Mews Am Dram production of Annie in nineteen-seventy-five and still maintains that it was the best chorus role anyone in the town has ever seen.

No, it were peaceful in the house without our Doris – more so than when she had laryngitis and used that bell and notepad to heckle me every five minutes. I brought my Daily Mirror inside and drank tea from a mug. I watched Groundforce and paused it whenever Charlie Dimmock lunged with a trowel. It were bliss. I didn't have to think about the garden safari and have our Doris ask if I think it's strange how Janice Dooley of Little Street and Doug Grey are always away at the same time.

Sometimes I wonder whether we're a bit unfair on Janice.

Then I remember she once tried to accost me in the Lidl car park. I don't know what I were more afraid of – our Doris finding out that Janice Dooley had tried it on, or our Doris finding out I'd parked at Lidl and walked into town because the car park were free.

Either way, Janice walked into a retractable bollard and got taken to casualty. I don't often agree with our Doris's vendetta but when it comes to Janice Dooley of Little Street, the entire town is in agreement.

I should have known my amnesty wouldn't last.

She'd only been gone for three hours when I received the phone call. When our Doris is here she goes all posh, likes to announce our address, surname and our names in case the caller were to get mistaken. She once had a cold caller hang up because she started harping on about how she'd used the same hairdresser since nineteen-eighty-five and she weren't sure she would recommend the use of foreign shampoo and conditioner and didn't the caller know that Doris had an Avon lady who saw to all of her cosmetic requirements?

So I were happy to answer the phone with a mild, 'hello' and didn't I hit a problem straight away. The familiar hush of breathing hissed down the receiver like a python with bronchitis. I heard her take a puff on her cigarette – imagined her thinking of what to have a go at first, my abysmal telephone manner or how I had treated our Doris. Because I knew who were calling all right. I have lived with our Doris for fifty four years – we have seen some horrible things together: gastroenteritis, kaftans, bomber jackets and Runcorn – and this woman, this thorn in my side has always been there to throw a spanner in the works.

Our Doris has a cousin, and her name is Mavis.

I first met Mavis when me and Doris were courting. I knew of her because the lads down the youth club used to say as if you wanted to get to Doris you had to get past her guard dog: Mavis. Now she's always been small has Mavis, has the look of one of those china dolls you keep in a glass cabinet – pity they ever let her out – I didn't make the best first impression if I'm honest, but I had no idea what she looked like.

Everyone said as she and Doris were like sisters, inseparable in looks and attitudes. Everyone must have been ruddy blind – either that or the entire town is charitable and if you saw the way they treated the youth choir you'd know that were a lie.

I were picking up our Doris for a trip to the pictures. I'd got my polo jumper on – the worst design ever known to man. If you ever want to strangle yourself, buy a polo jumper. I got to the front door and who answers but Mavis, yellow fingernails and a dodgy perm even in the sixties, and she gave me this look like a snake sizing up whether you'll fit in its mouth and she said to me, she said, 'I told Doris to see the optician but she didn't listen and now look at her, stepping out with a weasel in a neck brace – things must be low on the ground.' She then told me the tale of how our Doris could be with a jazz musician from Nether Alderley but he played on Friday nights.

I might've told her he'd clearly been scared off by the gargoyle on the front step as our Doris came into the hall.

And that's how it began; fifty four years of wedded bliss ... and Mavis.

Mavis who were on the other end of the phone, breathing like it were going out of fashion. And then she spoke, her words that pronounced she could have been the speaking clock, and she said, like it were news, like I hadn't noticed my lack of spouse, she said, 'Doris isn't at your house.'

And I knew where she'd gone. I said to her, and it were my long-standing hatred for Mavis that made me say, 'Do you know, Mavis, I hadn't noticed – I'd thought she were in the living room watching Alan Titchmarsh.'

'Now listen here, Harold Copeland, Doris is fed up of being abused by a Labour-worshipping, socialist layabout. Until you mend your ways she will be staying here with me.'

And I said, 'You can't teach an old dog new tricks – you should know that, your husband gave up trying.' And I put the phone down. I shouldn't have brought up her Percy but there were nothing I could do about it now I'd said it.

Besides I'd had enough of our Doris. The only reason she runs to Mavis is because they're both as selfish as each other. Doris never once asked whether I'd help her in the garden safari. I didn't mind doing it at first but that business with my shed was uncalled for. I thought, let her stay at Mavis's.

Since I had the phone in my hand, I did what any sensible man with free evening calls would do, I gave in and called the lads.

Alf arrived within the half hour, bottle of White Lightning under one arm and a six pack of pork pies beneath the other. 'I had a run to Tesco – only just escaped with me Melton Mowbrays. They're tightening security, 'arold.'

'It might be to stop the pensioners stealing their savoury goods.'

He said to me, he said, 'It's refrigerated.'

I rolled my eyes at that and pointed him in the direction of the fridge. Alf has always had a thing for nicking things – he'll never steal off his family, but he has got a thing about robbing pork pies. When we were lads we used to go to the Co-Op – our Doris had a way with a pricing gun that could make a younger Harold hot under the collar – and Alf couldn't help but stick his hands into the pick 'n mix. He's spent his life saying they let him off because no one noticed his pickpocketing prowess. I think they let him because they knew his uncle had a bad war – and they'd always get the money back one way or another; usually by overcharging him for the Christmas raffle down the Cricket Club.

Once Alf got himself acquainted with Doris's Brussels pâté – the kind she buys from the deli that has half the amount as Aldi but costs twice as much – the lads started showing up. Some brought drink, some brought turnips. It separates the men from the gardeners does a drink in our Doris's kitchen, it doesn't matter whether or not she's here.

Peter still weren't over our Doris stepping in his prized marrow. He couldn't speak to me for a few weeks after – I kept my head low, stuck to a brief nod of the head – he were more faithful to that marrow than he was to his wife. There were still that business between him and Cheryl from the Hare and Horse when they disappeared for two hours with a plate of haggis and a bottle of whisky at the Burns Night Celebrations, but that marrow, if that marrow got chilly he'd knit it a bleeding scarf.

And now he sat at the kitchen table, making fast work of a twelve pack of Skol on the table. I didn't blame him but I'm not sure a squashed marrow can merit alcoholism. I'm not the sort of man to stop another from his drunken endeavours. If there's anything I learnt from our Doris's mother it's that if you try and take their drink away, they'll find a new one after they've clouted you for taking theirs away in the first place.

I also wanted to join the lot of them – me and the allotment lads took the party to the living room. I switched the telly onto BBC so we could watch Alex Jones interview some up and coming about something we didn't care about. The One Show over and it were back to my recording of Charlie Dimmock. They might get some new young pieces on the telly but I always go back to the old favourites. Even as I sunk into one of Alf's pork pies I could hear our Doris making a fuss because of my objectification of women - that first night when we were at the flicks she caught me glancing at her breasts.

I said to her, I said, 'I'm a man, our Doris, I'm going to look at your breasts.'

And she said to me, she said, 'If you even want to get close to looking at my breasts then you'll stop treating me like a dirty magazine. I am a woman, 'arold Copeland, that doesn't give you the right to think my mammary glands were invented for your pleasure.' She made a point of buying her own popcorn and sitting three rows behind me; she left before the national anthem had finished playing and I had to stand through it. She had to wait for me because I'd brought her in my car but she didn't speak to me for three weeks afterward. It might have been Mavis, it might have been my objectification of the feminine form, I'm still not sure; it's only been fifty-four years, you've got to give a man a chance.

Once I couldn't stand up, I'm not sure what happened. I'm not denying that getting blind drunk two nights in a row is a bad thing – I'm not denying that I made some stupid choices and that I spent three hours the next morning worrying about my blood pressure and what Doris would say when she finally cottoned on to the loss of one of her Royal Doulton saucers.

The first time I ever broke one of our Doris's cups I thought she'd skin me alive.

We'd been married for seven years and our Doris had just served the afternoon tea to her friends from the ladies group. This were before the days of the church hall, they'd meet in the living room and discuss whether or not trifles could still be seen as a dessert in respectable society or whether they should be resigned to the underclasses who currently plagued the council development.

I were late home from work, something to do with a bad delivery of gnomes; they'd all been delivered with their feet on backwards – the manufacturer said as they had a dyslexic assistant on the line.

I found our Doris in the kitchen cleaning the crockery. She said to me, 'You're late.'

I said, 'I hadn't noticed, our Doris.'

She said, 'Don't get cheeky with me, our 'arold, what if you had been murdered? How would I explain that to the ladies group? You're not the kind of man who gets murdered on his way home from work.'

I said, 'I work at a garden centre, our Doris.'

'You're a purveyor of horticultural goods and don't you go around forgetting it in front of Violet Grey, that's all I need is her going on about how her husband is doing well at the factory. You could have gone on the line, you'd be manager by now.'

I shouldn't have mimicked her words but we'd had that conversation about fifty thousand times in the last three years and it always ended with me not being as good as Doug Grey.

It weren't the first time I'd received The Look but it were back in the early days before it had been properly refined, more of a squint that a proper burning gaze. And she said to me, all serious-like, clearly channelling her mother or a boarhound, she said, 'It would do to have some aspirations, our 'arold, just think about it – wouldn't you like it if we could retire to a nice cottage in the Cotswolds?'

I said I wouldn't and she threw the cup.

She missed.

The cup shattered and she said nothing. She collected the dustpan and brush from beneath the sink and cleared it up. Her silence spoke volumes. I spent the next three weeks getting in touch with manufacturers and wholesalers until I found the right match and even then she made me drink from a mug.

Anyway, I did my best at cleaning up the living room. I checked all the pots, vases, cupboards and drawers – anywhere someone could have thrown their guts up, I checked, and I found tons of vomit. I had to thank heavens for small mercies that they'd steered clear of the sofa. They might have felt the urge to throw up but at least they'd remembered whose house they were in and kept away from our Doris's upholstery.

I spent the best part of three hours going around the house cleaning; it weren't to a Doris standard but it would pass. And then I found Alf on the kitchen floor, our Doris's tablecloth around him like it were an eiderdown in the middle of winter, though it must have been cold against the hardwood flooring.

I had to bang a few plates around to wake him up.

And he didn't flinch. I said to him, I said, 'How can you be sober?'

'I lined my stomach,' he said.

'With pork pies.' I caught our Doris's tablecloth as he dropped it.

'Wi' Melton Mowbray, best there is.' One glance at the clock and he hopped out the back door, no thought to if I needed any help tidying up, but that's friends for you; there to help you make the mess but gone when you need to clear it.

Now I had to tackle the washing machine, and this is where I realised I hadn't used it since our Doris had me fork out the few hundred pounds for her top of the range washing machine in two-thousand-and-five. I said to myself, I said, 'You have lived with her for over half a century, a washing machine is child's play.'

I opened the drawer for the washing powder but we didn't have washing powder, we had some gunge that I had to squeeze into some sort of pot. I had to get my reading glasses out of the bedroom and then I realised I hadn't turned the bed over so I took the sheets back downstairs with me, and filled the machine to discover that you had to put the gunge in first – it explicitly says, first instruction, you can't miss it, and I'd done what anyone would do and put my washing in the washing machine before anything else. So, I had to take all of that out but then I didn't know what number you turned it to.

On the old machine it had been a four but our Doris wouldn't be happy if I shrunk her bed linen – she'd had them on order from British Home Stores, you could show them to your guests and they wouldn't think you were being too pretentious but on the right side of house proud; all Doris's idea. Personally, I don't care as long as I don't get bedsores.

I had no choice but to ring our Angela. She answered on the first ring, she said to me, she said, 'What's up, Dad?'

'How'd you know it were me?'

'Aunty Mavis rang.'

'She did, did she?'

'Yes, now what's up?'

She's nothing like her mother is our Angela, unless you count the middle-class views with a slight penchant for over-cleanliness but she knows how to look after her father does our Angela and I knew better than to pretend with her. I said to her, 'I can't work the washing machine.'

'You can't work the washing machine?'

'Your mother never lets me.'

'Is it turned on?'

And I can hear her smirking down the phone. I said to her, I said, 'It's no use laughing, our Angela, can you imagine the uproar if I mixed a colour with a white and destroyed one of your mother's Laura Ashley two-pieces.'

'You'd find it hard since she has them dry cleaned,' she said. 'Have you put the fabric softener in?'

'Is that the stuff that looks like something out of Ghostbusters?'

'I'm coming over, don't touch anything.'

Within the half hour, our Angela had set about the kitchen. She'd switched the washing machine on, made a brew and were just starting on the washing up when the doorbell went. I said I'd get it and lumbered down the hall. Not many folk visit us and if they do they're of the mind to ring first so I had no idea who it were until I saw the shadow through the frosted glass – the way she stood with her nose in the air like she were searching the heavens for something told me who she were.

I opened the door.

And there she stood. Violet Grey. I knew things were bad as soon as I laid eyes on her. I only ever see her at parties or supermarkets or that time she ran into the gents hoping to catch her husband at it. I don't know where he finds the energy for extra-marital affairs – he's getting on for seventy-six himself and he were the first to have a new knee.

And now his wife were on my doorstep.

She said to me, all pursed lips and saggy cheeks, 'Aren't you going to invite me in, Mr Copeland?'

I said to her, I said, 'Why?'

'For a chat,' she said.

'A chat?' I stepped to block the door. If our Doris knew as I'd let Violet Grey into a kitchen that were less than spotless, she'd have my dentures for a necklace. I said to Violet, I said, 'What could we have to chat about?'

And she said, all mock concern, as though the idea hadn't been percolating for the last three days, she said, 'Mrs Copeland's state of mind.'

'What about it?' I said.

And this is where she got cocky. She's more concerned about being top dog than our Doris's mental health. And she said, 'I believe the garden safari has become too stressful for Mrs Copeland – Doris – to handle. I wonder if it might be appropriate for her to rescind her application in order to preserve her state of mind.'

And that's where I thought my blood pressure would hit levels never seen in a white, suburban, middle-class male. Our Doris had told me what Violet Grey could be like but to hear it with my own two ears, to see her slightly lop-sided smirk was another matter entirely. I said, 'You'd like that wouldn't you? Our Doris is off at her cousin's and you're thinking, "I'm too much of a coward to offend her face to face, I'll go through her husband instead." Well last I heard, Mrs Grey, you'd stepped down as chair of the safari to stop your husband copping off with other birds and I suggest you get back to it whilst our Doris puts on the biggest school reunion this town has ever seen!'

I slammed the door in her face before the 'well I never' but I were shaking, partly because of Violet Grey and partly because I now had to arrange a Doris-standard school reunion.

Our Angela came in from the kitchen and said to me, she said, 'What was that all about, Dad?'

I said, 'Get the lads on the phone, Angela.'

She walked away and I hoped beyond hope they weren't paralytic.

It took them the best part of two hours but soon enough they'd reassembled themselves in the front room, mugs of coffee in their hands, looking worse for the wear. I stood there hoping I were giving off the impression of a leader rather than a man under threat from his wife. I said to them, I said, 'Right lads I know our Doris ain't really flavour of the month but I've had Violet Grey on my doorstep and I've made some promises on our Doris's behalf so I need your help.'

'What sort of promises?' Peter piped up. He were just managing to keep his head out of the mop bucket.

'He's promised a school reunion my Mum would approve of.' Our Angela said, arms folded; she can be as domineering as her mother can that one, 'And I know that she can be a bit heavy-handed at times but can you imagine how she might react if she found out about the mess you left her house in this morning?'

Alf said, 'You wouldn't tell her would you, Angela?'

She said, and this is where I were proud of her, she'd deployed our Doris as she were meant to be deployed: a weapon, and it had put the fear of God in them, she said, 'It depends on whether you can bring a buffet and guests to the church hall.'

The lads looked white, the threat of our Doris finding out how we'd used her home hung in the air like cow muck in the countryside. Peter said, he said, 'How long do we have?'

Angela said, 'Tonight.' She must have noticed the

look of terror on my face; it were as though I'd discovered a grenade beneath the petunias and didn't know how to get it out before it made a mess of our Doris's paving, because Angela looked at me and she said, 'I've had a phone call, she's coming home.'

My heart entered my stomach, my mouth went dry as a Tory in the Gobi Desert and I said, 'She's going to kill me,' as Alf said, 'We'll help. On the condition she doesn't find out we had any hand in the preparation.'

Angela nodded. 'Done.'

'Then let's get to work.'

I've never seen them move as fast, not even when Eleanor Stockwell's skirt caught on a bit of netting and exposed her right buttock to a load of toddlers at the summer fête. Alf said as he'd get set on the refreshments and Peter said he'd go home and get some stuff. One of the lads asked if we needed any crockery but this is a point I was adamant on, I said to him, I said, 'If our Doris sees any crockery that is not her own at the school reunion then she will tear out our spleens and make a stew to bring to the ladies group. I'll sort crockery, you get on organising the church hall.'

'She'll want bunting,' our Angela added as an afterthought.

She would and all. Our Doris has a thing about bunting, says as it is a truly British decoration and the fact it can be achieved from a few scraps of fabric means it's economic which is exactly what we need in this day and age. I wish she'd been as thrifty about the dress she bought for our thirtieth wedding anniversary.

Me and our Angela set about finding the crystal champagne flutes and crockery for the tea and coffee. She went off to the church hall and I went to find my suit. Our Doris says as black doesn't suit my skin tone, says as I look like an anaemic Dracula, which is why I have the navy blue suit.

The navy suit has stood me in good stead. When our Richard were getting married for the fifth time, our Doris had me buy it from Marks. Since then it's been to three Christenings, one more of Richard's weddings and several funerals, one of them being Richard's. It's the only suit our Doris hasn't had thrown away after the second wear – usually they'd be at the charity shop by now. Sometimes I like to think it's because she's finally accepting me for who I am, but I think it's to do with the price of her last fur coat.

Once I were dressed our Angela came back and said to me, she said, 'Make sure you apologise to her, Dad. Grovel, do whatever you have to because I'm not sure we can cope with any more of her madcap schemes.'

I said to her, I said, 'There's Christmas yet, our Angela.'

She said, 'Don't remind me,' and we left.

It took a few minutes to get to the church hall and the whole time I could feel my heart pumping that fast I thought it had finally come: karma had caught up with me and I was being punished for offending our Doris. In that moment I were thinking a cardiac arrest might be more appealing than our Doris's face on seeing the church hall half done. We only had a dozen old aged pensioners trying to do what our Doris would normally spend months organising.

The ladders were out and a few of the lad's families had stepped into help. We had young folk tying bunting to the ceiling and others setting up trestle tables for the buffet. Thankfully someone had reminded them that our Doris preferred the trestle tables because they emphasised that the church was in need of funding as well as making sure that everyone knew she had better furnishings back at home but she couldn't possibly accommodate so many in her small lounge. Not that she would ever complain about her house on Shakespeare Avenue.

After six hours of work the church hall looked magnificent. Well, it looked as well as church halls can look. The lights were dimmed to an appropriate level; our Doris has a thing about dimmed lights at parties, says as if she'd wanted to have entertained in the dark she'd have become a lady of the night, but she still maintains there's something to be said for a light that casts the right hue over your guests so as you can't see every crevice on their face.

A few of Alf's acquisitions were on the buffet table: Melton Mowbray pork pies, sausage rolls, a few trays of pâté and Jacob's crackers, he'd even gone as far as to get a few Thornton's chocolates and piled Ferrero Rocher on top of each other – our Doris still maintains that Ferrero Rocher have something of a vintage quality about them that causes parties to become more of a social event but I think it's because she's always had a thing for hazelnuts.

Peter had brought a few bottles of his elderflower wine; they now sat alongside the bottles of Lambrusco and Shloer that Alf had managed to procure, no doubt from some off-the-back-of-a-truck source his Edith wouldn't be too pleased to hear about.

A whole host of folk filled the church hall. Old Ernie Oswaldthwaite sat with his missus throwing back the gin and tonics like they were Alka-Seltzers. I thought Yvonne Ackersley had emigrated, that Tabitha Quail had died but there they were, dancing around their handbags like they used to down the Rugby Club when they were lasses; Tabitha had something of a limp about her so her twist looked more like she were trying to readjust her knickers but it didn't matter because she were enjoying herself.

We were all enjoying ourselves.

And in the cloak room, I saw her shrugging off her coat. Our Doris.

She walked into the hall and stood there, a twinkle in her eye that could have been the glitter ball or cataracts and it didn't matter because she looked a million dollars – starling silhouettes on her white dress and her hair freshly permed and she had this come hither look, the like of which I hadn't seen since bonfire night of nineteen-ninety-four when I set fire to an effigy of Carly Simon.

I went over and she said to me, she said, 'It's come to my attention that you offended Violet Grey's birdwatching, our 'arold.'

And I said, 'I know nothing about any birdwatching but I had a go at her.'

'Our Angela says as you can't work the washing machine – I'll have to teach you something, we can't have it getting out that Doris Copeland's husband doesn't know how to work a spin cycle.'

'I look forward to it.'

Janice Dooley of Little Street approached with a pint of ale in one hand and a vol-au-vent in the other. She'd had a go at applying fake eyelashes and ended up looking like she'd glued moths to her eye lids. Her perfume were a mixture of Carlsberg and Dove deodorant. She and our Doris faced each other like the final showdown in a Western; I could feel folk stealing glances across the hall, wondering whether they'd get a repeat of the great slanging match of New Years nineteen-sixty-seven when Janice met our Doris in the Gadsden and Taylor car park.

But this were tame.

This were courteous.

This were political.

Janice started. She said to our Doris, she said, 'I'm right sorry, Doris, but I can't let you have a place on the garden safari. I'm thinking of you, really, I am.'

Our Doris looked every bit the hen with her back straight and nose in the air, she spoke slow, drawling out her words, she said, 'And how might that be?' You know things are bad when our Doris slows down her speech; when Mrs Carsley told her she'd seen a pinafore that matched Doris's at Aldi her speech slowed down that much I worried she'd had a stroke.

'I think the stress would be too much, you being seventy-two, after all.'

'I should imagine it's more stressful trying to keep your extra-marital endeavours a secret,' our Doris said.

'Now that's gossiping, Doris, you're hurt.' Janice swigged from her pint thinking she were in command of the situation.

'All the stress of keeping this from my dear friend Violet.'

'She knows.'

Our Doris brought out the Look, her eyes beaded, leaning in close to Janice as she hissed, 'I imagine she does but if you want me to keep quiet you'll give me fifth house. You'd prefer the public to know about my horticultural skills than what Violet Grey lets her husband get up to.'

'How do you know they're not splitting up?'

'And risk the scandal? I knew you were a few

sandwiches short of the full picnic, Janice but I thought that even you might understand why you and Doug aren't sipping cocktails in the Seychelles.' Our Doris held her head high, every inch the Head Girl as she said, 'Violet would never have given you the safari if it weren't for you and Doug so fifth house or the Gazette hears all about how Janice Dooley of Little Street should be awarded a Guinness World Record for the speed she can drop her knickers.'

I could practically hear the cogs whirring in Janice's head as she said, 'I'll see what I can do.' She lumbered off, vol-au-vent crushed in her hand.

I turned to our Doris and said to her, I said, 'That were brilliant.'

'Vol-au-vents, 'arold, really? Even Iceland were aware that they're a pitiful excuse for a buffet.'

4

TEETH

Our Doris has never been one for dentures. She is proud of the fact that she is one of three members of the Partridge Mews Women's Institute who still has her own teeth and has never had a filling. It's not for want of trying, mind you. We used to go to this dentist in town: Mr Alderson, he was NHS, our Doris won't go private because she's worried about funding an illegal immigrant's ingrown toenail surgery.

Now he weren't a young man himself, Alderson, but our Doris doesn't go in for ageism. She were fond of his practice and Royal Doulton tea set in a vintage 1950's sideboard. She's always had a thing for pine furniture, said it were a sturdy wood but was only really suited to farm dwellings, or small town dental practices.

Mr Alderson's room were nothing short of a cubby hole. Before this dreaded day she called it cosy and said how being close to your dental professional gave a sense of comfort, she said at least there were no space to fondle you. Well, Mr Alderson got our Doris in his chair. Mantovani were playing in the background – our

Doris insisted on bringing her own tape because she couldn't have it going around that she listened to BBC Radio 2. Alderson were there, churning out numbers to the dental nurse when he decided to find a cavity.

He looked at our Doris like something from The Wind in the Willows. He were all ginger and he said to her, he said, 'You're going to need a filling, Mrs Copeland.'

Our Doris moved that fast she knocked the floating light into the nurse's head. Our Doris were seething, all beetle eyes and sucked lips, she said to Alderson, she yelled, 'Who do you think you are to go spreading rumours like that?'

'You have a cavity, Mrs Copeland,' Alderson repeated, clearly a man who hadn't learnt to play dead when faced by a bear.

'I have a cavity? Have you heard him, our 'arold?' I have a cavity.' She turned on him at that point and said to him, she said, 'I'll give you a cavity in your bleeding great forehead in a minute.'

The nurse piped up at this and said, 'We will not tolerate violence towards our staff.'

'Violence? Violence! He wants to drill into my teeth and you call me violent? You're making it up so you can charge me extra. Sitting there thinking that because I am a heterosexual white women with Conservative leanings and a penchant for floral blouses from the British Home Stores that you can charge me an extortionate amount for a bit of tin foil on my molar!' She bundled her coat in her arms, something she wouldn't usually do because she'd bought it from the boutique for eighty pounds and she warned against flashing your size labels at anyone in case they used it against you to your circle of friends.

She faced Mr Alderson, and she said to him, she said, 'I'm afraid that the state of your practice is in need of a spring clean. There is a certain air of damp and I'm not sure I can support a dental practice where there is a definite sense of menace and underhand goings-on. From now on I and my family shall see Mrs Patel of Tudor Dwelling.'

He closed within a year. Our Doris intimated that he was no good to the WI, who removed their families. The rumour mill started up and a young lass of the council estate claimed her son's milk teeth wouldn't have fallen out so early if she hadn't been to Mr Alderson. He ended up moving to Prestatyn with the vicar and opening a Bed and Breakfast – they adopted a cat.

That were a few decades ago. Our Doris must've got word around somehow. She never did get that filling, but she has chipped a tooth. You'd think that after seventy-two years she'd know you can't bite straight into a strawberry bon-bon. I warned her, I did, I said to her, I said, 'Your teeth are buggered as it is, our Doris, you can't just crunch straight in – it's not a liquorice torpedo.'

And that's when she gave me The Look, she scrunched her brow, opened the bag and with one, 'Watch me,' dove right in. There was a crack – her eyes went from pinched to gawping – and she had a moment of realisation.

No, you can't bite straight into a strawberry bon-bon.

She opened her mouth and spat out the sweet and half an incisor. Fury pooled on her lips and I thought to myself, ''arold, you're a dead man.'

I could see the headlines – wife kills husband for

knowing too much. Our Doris screamed like I'd never heard her scream before – even in childbirth she was too busy wondering what shade of mauve to wear to the christening to let out a serious whimper.

One chipped tooth and I knew I was done for – there'd be no need for a casket, our Doris was going to eat me alive.

She opened her mouth till her jaw cracked and yelled at me, I'm positive she yelled, 'Look at what you've gone and done, our 'arold. Seventy-two years of age, no dentures – never had a cavity and you come along and dare me to eat a bon-bon. What will Marcia at Number Forty-Two think when she sees me? What am I going to do?' I held back all tooth fairy comments, and rang the dentist.

Our Doris hadn't been sat there a minute when Mrs Patel hit her with the bombshell, she said to her, she said, 'I'm afraid I'll have to extract the tooth, Mrs Copeland.'

I thought our Doris were going to throw a fit. I started glancing around, looking for somewhere I might be able to hide. I were sat at the kiddies table, were considering flipping it on its side and making a shield when our Doris piped up with, 'That is quite all right, Mrs Patel, I trust you completely. One must, you know, in these uncertain times. However, I would like to pose the question as to how you will endeavour to replace the offending incisor. I have been invited to the Antiques Roadshow by Miss Janice Dooley of Little Street.'

And I could see the cogs whirring in Mrs Patel's mind. Most folk are aware of how to deal with our Doris – she's high maintenance but once you do as she wants you're sorted. Only I didn't think Mrs Patel would ever be sorted. She said to our Doris, she said, 'There's always the possibility of veneers or a crown but honestly your tooth has an incredible infection. I'm surprised you haven't noticed something before.'

'I come from a long line of ancestors with high pain thresholds. My grandfather once played a rather smashing round of golf with a dislocated shoulder. Granted he almost decapitated the coach of the women's volleyball team but these are occupational hazards.'

'It will require a fair amount of work – I cannot guarantee you'll have your crown by the Antiques Roadshow.'

'It is a week away, Mrs Patel, I'm quite sure you'll have an adequate amount of time in which to service my teeth.'

After that Mrs Patel reached for the local anaesthetic and kept quiet.

Our Doris's pain threshold didn't last as far as the needle penetrating her gum. She wailed at Mrs Patel like a banshee giving birth to a ten ton kidney stone. Her hands clenched the arms of the chair and her toes curled more than they ever did when we got amorous.

Mrs Patel finished and our Doris sat there, her face sagging a little, the temporary crown stark white against her other teeth. I were glad she were off her face because if she'd seen herself she'd have torn it out and used it as a weapon.

When we got home our Doris fell down onto the sofa with all the pomp of an inebriated hippopotamus. I said to her, I said, 'Do you fancy a brew, our Doris?' and she told me as her fifth cousin twice removed on her father's side had a thing for Special Brew and she'd always wondered about the flavour.

I hadn't the heart to tell her I meant PG Tips.

Once the anaesthetic had worn off a bit, she started poking and prodding the crown with her tongue. I could see her there like Eddie Sykes trying to hide a gobstopper in Mr Morris's class but threatening our Doris with a slipper wouldn't do much good so I said to her, I said, 'You should stop messing with the crown, our Doris.'

And she said to me, more of a drawl than anything, she said, 'I'm not doing anything.'

I said, 'I can see you.'

And she said, 'You couldn't see Eleanor Stockwell's knickers when she flashed them at the summer fête, you most certainly cannot see me pressing my tongue against my teeth.'

'Well not now you're talking,' I said.

I thought she'd rip out my jugular but she sat back in the sofa and said to me, she said, 'Do make a mug of tea, 'arold, I could do with a drop of rum – for purely medicinal purposes of course.'

'Should you be having alcohol?'

'Should you be questioning it?'

I had the Captain Morgan out of the drinks cabinet when the phone rang. Before I could get to the hall, the slurred dulcet tones of our Doris spurred to life with, 'Good afternoon, you have reached Mrs Doris Copeland of twenty-two Shakespeare Avenue – oh, hello, Angela. The orthodontist?'

I reached the lounge to see that look in our Doris's eyes – not the one that expresses that you've raised the fury of seven hells in her, but the one she gets when she's thinking about something, considering how what she's been told could be used to her advantage; it's why it took her three days to accept when I proposed.

The best part of an hour passed before our Doris got off the phone. I went into her and said, I said, 'What's our Angela got to say for herself then?'

'We're taking Theo to the orthodontist tomorrow morning. It's half term so he's the day off school, I thought perhaps we could take him for a spot of lunch at the Hare and Horse. Did you forget about my tea? Honestly, 'arold, I thought you might have it ready by now.'

Next day I sat in the car park waiting for our Doris to get back with Theo. She'd left me with the copy of The Times I kept stashed in the glove compartment in case our Doris came along for the ride; I change it every few weeks. She went to visit her Aunty Phyllis once – Mavis's mother; we never got on – I might have said, and I were a bit squiffy on sherry trifle at the time, I said, 'I can see where the gargoyle gets it from, her mother's as stony faced as Ben Nevis.'

I weren't invited back.

And now Phyllis were on her death bed and if I didn't want to see her living, I most certainly didn't want to see her dead. Mavis'd start telling folk that the sight of me was enough to shock her mother to death, and she's got friends in the right places has Mavis, I'd be imprisoned before the funeral; forget All Things Bright and Beautiful, I'd be singing for my supper.

Our Doris must have been by Aunty Phyllis's side for eleven hours. I fiddled with the different knobs on the radio, discovered a station that played Pam Ayres on repeat, heard Richard Tauber at one point and weren't that a blast from the past? When I needed to empty my bladder I knew I were beggared; I couldn't mosey on up to the house and ask whether I could relieve myself. I had to hold it. I considered letting it go and claiming incontinence but I know that our Doris would bury me alive if I let myself go in a jacket from John Lewis. I dozed off at one point, only to be awoken by our Doris planting her fist on the horn. She said to me, she said, 'I can't believe you'd be so disrespectful, our 'arold, I know you didn't get on but there's no need to sit outside her house looking untidy.'

And that's when I decided to keep a newspaper in the car. I considered putting National Geographics in the motor after that but I knew that she wouldn't settle for anything less than The Times. She isn't that happy about me reading the newspaper in the car as it is – calls it common and says as I could at least pretend to be interested in the world around me –but she'll let it slide as long as I'm reading a newspaper she has approved.

I only had to wait about half an hour before they were back in the car. Theo had his shoulders hunched and I knew something were up. I know teenage boys are meant to go around being loutish – with the possibility of breaking into the allotment and uprooting me petunias – but our Theo isn't like that, partly because of his grandmother, and partly because he's never been one for getting filthy.

Our Doris, meanwhile, had her head held high, although she did have a scarf wrapped around her mouth. I considered gagging her years ago but I always worried someone might see it as sexual rather than an act of humanitarianism.

Theo sat down in the back and stared straight ahead as our Doris got into the car.

I said to him, I said, 'How'd it go?'

He spoke slow – I think he's learnt that if you want our Doris to take you seriously you have to speak in slow and measured tones. I tell you, if he already knows how to speak to Doris, he'll be Prime Minister one day. He said to me, he said, 'She is never bringing me again.'

I looked at our Doris and I said, 'What happened?'

Her words were muffled behind the scarf but she said to me, she said, 'The orthodontist and I might have had a mild disagreement.'

I flashed a glance at Theo in the back and said, 'We'll talk about this over dinner.'

At the Hare and Horse, whilst our Doris were using the facilities, I said to Theo, I said, 'What happened?'

He launched into a right tale, he said, 'He'd just tightened my braces when Nan piped up with, "I wonder if you'd mind taking a look at my teeth, only I saw a dentist yesterday and she says I need a crown, would it be possible for you to offer specialist, alternative advice?" She's lost a tooth, not an iPhone and Mr Shepherd said, "I'm afraid I have another appointment after this, but if you speak to my receptionist I'm sure I could squeeze you in." Is that enough for my grandmother though? No. Some people get grandparents who are good enough to be senile and who do I get? Mrs Doris Copeland.'

I said to him, I said. 'What did she do?'

He sipped at his bitter shandy like most young lads do; he wanted a drink but he weren't that impressed with the flavour.

'She went ballistic, she said, "Do you believe the NHS was merely invented for youth with dental crookedness? I had a bowl cut until I was seventeen, I understand these matters. My grandson is here as a patient, all I am asking is that you take the simplest glance at my teeth and then we will be on my way." He couldn't help her, Grandad, there was a girl from Saint Ormerod's waiting to have headgear removed.'

I choked back a snigger and said, 'I'm supposing it didn't end there.'

Theo shook his head. 'She said that she's got the Antiques Roadshow coming up and did he think she could do that looking like a hillbilly. What's she talking about Antiques Roadshow?'

'It's to raise the profile of the garden safari,' I said, 'Janice Dooley of Little Street is going on with a vase she found in her mother's loft.'

'Why's Nan not taking anything?'

I said to him, I said, 'The oldest thing about our house is your grandmother.'

'She's younger than you,' he said.

I said, 'You're not wrong there.'

The truth is that when our Doris found out the Antiques Roadshow is coming to the leisure centre, she went on a raid of the house. She were determined, she put curry in her Tupperware so it would appear aged. She never used them, maintains that Tupperware is the sign that one has eyes too big for their belly – one should never waste as much as to warrant the use of Tupperware; still she believed that an authentic, used Tupperware dish might elicit some emotional reaction from someone.

She got it into her head that her cutlery had stamps on them.

I said to her, I said, 'When in fifty-four years of marriage have we ever afforded silver cutlery, our Doris, there were a time we couldn't even afford paper cups.'

She held a finger to her lips and said to me, she said, 'If you think that we have not been able to afford something as simple as cutlery, our 'arold then how come we could buy a shed that blocks my view of Mrs Witstanley's garden?'

I left it at that and she hopped off to the jewellers. When she came back her face had shrunk in on itself – if I hadn't known better I'd have said she'd swallowed a lemon. She dropped her bags and moaned, she said, 'Bleeding jeweller couldn't tell gold from corn flakes – I would've given him what for if it hadn't been for the antiques.'

And that's when I noticed the newspaper, I asked her, I said, 'You get the Gazette sent to you, our Doris, what are you going after buying it for?'

She shook her head and flashed the front page. There she stood in all her glory, wearing a gold blazer beside the headline that proclaimed she had found an antique. I didn't have time to read it myself before our Doris exclaimed, she said, 'Janice Dooley of Little Street has discovered an antique vase she believes could be from the Ming Dynasty. If she hasn't had it as hush money from Violet Grey, I'd be surprised.'

She should have taken her teeth, they're the most antique thing she owns.

At the pub, our Doris returned with her scarf pinned around her mouth. When Linda brought the food over our Doris said to her she said, 'This scarf is not a religious statement, I believe I am developing a sore throat and do not wish to aggravate it.'

Linda nodded her head and went off to give Mrs Butterworth her port and lemon.

I said to our Doris, I said, 'What are you saying things like that for – you know she'll tell everyone next chance she has.'

Our Doris nodded, a glint in her eye, she said to

me, she said, 'I should hope she does – I can't have it getting around that I am in need of a crown. I doubt that orthodontist can keep his mouth shut, lord knows he didn't whilst we were there. Asking me about my Bonfire Night – there's a reason the hall is exclusive, you know?'

When we got home me and Theo went into the lounge and our Doris checked her messages and set about the telephone. I'm glad I don't get to look at the phone bill anymore because even with free calls I'm confident the cost would turn my blood pressure to rocket fuel.

The Countdown conundrum were just flashing across the screen when our Doris walked in, scarf hanging from her shoulders, eyes wild – she'd bypassed the Look by that far I'm not sure she knew what her eyes were doing. She said, more of a roar than anything, and she said to us, 'You'll never believe what she's gone and done, our 'arold. I should have known she'd do something like this, it's typical, I don't know why I didn't anticipate it.'

Theo piped up with, 'Who?'

I shrank back into my armchair as our Doris's tirade continued, she said, 'Janice has only gone and had the Antiques Roadshow moved to this Saturday. Apparently it's more convenient for the television crew – that bleeding orthodontist must have let it slip. Has he never heard of the Hippocratic oath? Where's my patient confidentiality?'

'You weren't his patient, our Doris,' I said.

'I saw his hands, do you think I'd let him anywhere near my mouth?'

Theo's hands were in his mouth faster than Alf pocketing a pork pie. 'You let him near mine.'

'You're young, your body is made to fight infection. I'm going to have to get in touch with Pandra, she'll circulate the rumour that I have an issue with my throat and by the time it reaches Janice Dooley it'll be laryngitis.' Our Doris applauded herself and stopped.

I said to her, I said, 'What's wrong?'

'I can't, 'arold, this is meant to secure our place as fifth house. We'll get Mrs Patel on the phone, I'm sure it won't take too long for her to replace this monstrosity.' And with that our Doris revealed the white fang that jutted from her mouth like a crag from a mountain range.

Mrs Patel couldn't help her. I were in the garden the next morning digging up my calla lilies when our Doris stormed down the path, leaving her bag at the back door. Her scarf was back in place, her words muffled as she said to me, she said, 'Do you know what Mrs Patel said? She told me that her technician didn't work that fast, I said, it's a matter of urgency but did I get anywhere? Me, a heterosexual home-owner? Did I buggery – her hygienist wouldn't be much use to a rugby team.'

I went back to my gardening and our Doris went to write a letter to the Gazette about how the Antiques Roadshow had helped to raise the profile of a small town women's institute.

Saturday came and our Doris made us wait outside the leisure centre whilst she readjusted a floral scarf she felt accompanied her cream Bon Marche blazer quite appropriately for an upper middle class event. She said to me, she said, 'If this isn't a Ming Dynasty vase, our 'arold, I'm going to make sure Janice Dooley never leaves bleeding Little Street.'

I straightened my tie, followed her inside and said to her, I said, 'I bet you will, our Doris.'

A television crew filled the leisure centre. Our Doris found Pandra and they went to stand, seemingly in the crowd but close enough to Janice to make an impression. I joined the other husbands in the doorway, Eddie had snuck in a pick 'n' mix and a hip flask. We made our coffees Irish and settled down to watch our wives do what they did best.

The vase were huge. You'd expect to see it on a show like this, or Downton Abbey or one of those ones where folk send stuff to auction. I were almost glad that our Doris didn't bring her Tupperware, she'd have become one of those jokes, like that lady who took in the gold dust and it turned out to be paint. She should've sent the video into You've Been Framed, at least she'd have earned two-hundred-and-fifty quid.

I couldn't really hear what went on but Janice spent the first two minutes smiling and telling a story. Once the presenter started talking, her face fell. It were like watching someone having a stroke before your eyes — that'd be a first for television an OAP dropping down dead on the Antiques Roadshow.

I didn't have to wait for long to find out what happened.

Our Doris practically skipped back over to me. Her scarf had slipped and revealed her fang. She were that happy she linked arms with me.

I said to her, I said, 'What's gotten into you, our Doris?'

'You'll never believe it, 'arold! It's not a Ming Dynasty vase.'

'I thought you said you'd make her stay in Little Street,' I said.

She said, 'I had to leave, 'arold, I could have wet myself laughing. Pandra's had Geoff take her down the pub.'

'So what is it?'

'A bit of old tat they used to sell back in the seventies – apparently everyone and their cousin had one. I wouldn't, did you see it? Can you imagine that in a provincial semi-detached house in Shakespeare Avenue?'

'You flashed your crown, our Doris.'

She must have been high off something because she said to me, she said, 'Yes, my crown, 'arold, I've always thought I could be royalty.'

'It's part of your tooth,' I said.

'It doesn't matter where it is. I have it, and it's a damn sight more impressive than that vase, I can tell you.'

5

THE LAST WALTZ

Our Doris has taken to listening to rock music.

It's an act of rebellion after our grandson Theo said as he won't dance with her at the Christmas party. Every year at the church hall the ladies group throw a Christmas party; they round up their families and like cattle we're ushered away from the final of Strictly Come Dancing to eat uncooked vegetables smothered in lukewarm gravy. I mentioned it to our Doris, I did, I said to her, 'My fixadent can't handle these carrots.'

And she said, 'They're al dente, 'arold.'

'I don't care whether they're bleeding Al Capone, they're going to break my dentures,' I said.

My complaints went unheeded. No matter, the DJ turned up the music – the ladies group started to vet the DJs after the last one decided to play the Cha Cha Slide. He said as it was an effort to get the kids to get up and dance. Violet Grey said as it was nothing short of debauchery and he would never work in this town again. He's got another gig on the local radio so he's not doing too badly for himself.

When the music comes on all of the old 'uns get up and start dancing. Well it were all we had to do when we were younger, apart from funny business behind the youth club and in winter it were better to contend with the twist than chilblains. Only now they're not twisting but waltzing across the room.

I think our Theo were four when he first started on about dancing. He'd seen Angela and Neil having a go and must've thought he'd like to have a bash. Well if our Doris didn't immediately set about our Angela for not having her son signed up for dance classes at such a late stage in life. She said to our, Doris, Angela said, 'He's only just out of pull-ups, Mum, he won't be much good at quick step.'

It didn't take our Doris ten minutes to arrange for Theo to start dancing lessons with Heather Yearly; she had the cheque book after all. He's done all sorts of competitions since then has our Theo and each year he's taken our Doris to the dance floor to perform a dance they spend the best part of four months getting right.

Ten years later, he doesn't want to.

And our Doris is heartbroken.

I knew there were something wrong when we went to do a spot of Christmas shopping. The majority had already been done, these were gifts for those our Doris didn't particularly mind forgetting about. For the first time in years she had to get Janice Dooley of Little Street something other than a Card Factory card with 'from the Copelands' scrawled beneath the Happy Christmas.

The select few she does like get home-made cards; a depiction of a gingerbread house in the background, with decoupage of two holly berries, and an appropriate amount of glitter that isn't too gaudy but exudes the correct impression required to truly appreciate the festive season. She starts making them in April.

We went into Boots to find something for Janice. Our Doris usually thinks about these things for months in advance, knows what a gift says about the person receiving it and the person giving it, so as not to make any social faux pas. I'd asked our Doris to see the list and was told, in no uncertain terms, that I wouldn't get a look at her list. She told me, she said to me, 'If I even so much as think that you have glanced at the Christmas list, our 'arold, it won't be turkey getting roasted for dinner, I can tell you.'

Our Doris took the list from the pocket of her duffel coat. She brought the folded list up to her lips and inched it open before stealing one peek and rushing it back into her pocket.

I said to her, I said, 'You look like you're on a kamikaze mission, our Doris.'

She said, 'All purchases can and will be used against you. Honestly, 'arold, I thought you knew that – look what happened when Jif became Cif.' Then she sped off down the aisle.

Boots at Christmas is like stepping into Jesus's stable – overcrowded and someone's stepped in foreign muck. Folk tend to see our Doris coming and step aside, probably because they know she's not afraid to beat them with her handbag; not at Christmas anyway. She keeps a special handbag for Christmas – plain black, faux leather from Marks and Spencer. Our Doris found the aisle she needed, without having to wield her handbag, and froze. She turned to me, eyes wide, barely a lash away from the Look and she said, 'They're out of stock.'

I said, 'I thought you didn't mind about getting Janice a gift.'

She said, 'This wasn't for Janice, it's for Theo.'

I stopped and took notice of what were on the shelves and I thought our Theo wouldn't go for much of this; the shelves were full to the brim with anti-aging creams, lotions, pills and in one case a glove that when wiped across the face would miraculously remove wrinkles. I said to her, I said, 'I don't think Theo would go in for Oil of Olay, our Doris, he's only fourteen.'

The Look weren't prominent but there was a definite sign of lip trembling and she said to me, all deflated, she said, 'He won't dance with me because I'm old, our 'arold, look at me – would any man want to dance with a seventy-two year old woman?'

I said to her, I said, 'I'd love to dance with you, our Doris.'

And she said, 'You're obligated to, 'arold, we're married, I don't want someone to dance with me just because they're obligated.'

I had to employ some of that quick thinking I'd got used to using over the last fifty-four years. I thought back to the time she lost an earring in Edinburgh and said to her, I said, 'Come on, let's go for a coffee.'

Normally she'd protest that she doesn't like coffee bars and that we should be supporting local businesses but she simply nodded her head and dallied back to the front door, shoulders slumped and head downcast.

We took window seats at the coffee shop, with a view of the town Christmas tree. It's a spectacle that our Doris has had a thing for since we were first courting. That first December I brought her to town in the middle of the night; we were all bundled up in scarves and gloves and turtleneck jumpers cutting off our circulation. And our Doris were a different person, seeing that Christmas tree were an epiphany as though all that were good in the world could be found in the needles.

There's a stable scene with Mary, Joseph and the baby surrounded by shepherds and the three kings. They were carved and painted by some of the lads from the allotment and Pete fitted some lights to match the ones they've strung down the main street. Our Doris stared out the window for a few minutes, just looking at the tree, her face set with some sort of determination and I were sure she were on the edge of tears.

I didn't press the issue. I drank my coffee without comments about how the low-lighting made it impossible to see anything. She watched the scene around the Christmas tree. Children milled about behind the gate, pointing at the baby Jesus and altogether getting excited about the whole thing. Our Doris used to pass comment on the intermingling of Christ and Santa Claus in popular culture, but she didn't.

After a few minutes she turned to me and said, she said, 'I know that he's fourteen, and I did expect him to stop dancing with me one day, but I thought I'd have some warning, our 'arold, I'd have liked to have known that the last dance would have been our grand finale.'

I said to her, 'You'd have treated it like a last dance, our Doris, it wouldn't have had the same splendour.'

She slurped her coffee as though the barista might have added a measure of poison and said, 'Imagine the fun Violet Grey's going to have with the news – my own grandson won't dance with me.'

'You shouldn't take it to heart, our Doris,' I said.

It didn't do much good. When we got home the rock music started. We have some tapes from when Angela were dating a drummer. She'd be in her room for hours listening to the tapes at full whack; our Doris thought it were fantastic that she had a wayward daughter she could use to escape social engagements. If Angela wanted to go to a Billy Idol concert our Doris got out of going to Mrs Witstanley's Book Club; dull due to Jilly Cooper and the second hand gossip.

I hadn't known our Doris enjoyed the music as well.

I'd been down to the allotment. We don't do much in winter, but the boss man can get us some cheap vegetables from the farmer's market and our wives love nothing more than telling folk that they use only locally sourced produce for their Christmas dinners. Our Doris spent three months harping on about Brussel sprouts once, she only stopped because a topless Deborah Osmond were caught driving recklessly on a one way system; she claimed underwire, the Gazette called it exhibitionism.

I had my hands full with bags of carrots, sprouts and potatoes and some booze our Doris had asked me to get in case Alf wanted something more than the wine she'd already brought to accompany her veritable feast of festive frivolity.

As I walked up the front path I heard the drums thundering and the guitars screaming and men singing lyrics that full of supposed debauchery I were surprised our Doris had let them anywhere near her stereo. I went inside and took the bags through to the kitchen. I saw her sat in the lounge as I passed, staring straight ahead as she made paper garlands.

I said to her, I said, 'Do you fancy a brew, our

Doris?'

She said to me, 'Meat Loaf.'

I said, 'What?'

'Don't say what, it's Meat Loaf,' she said and went back to her garlands. We don't put our decorations up until the twelfth and even then our Doris saves decorations for the main event, when she invites a specially selected group of family and friends to partake in a Christmas feast – I'd ordered the turkey from the farm shop in June. I didn't have a weight, or measurements, our Doris went all happy Ebenezer and told me to order the biggest they had.

I didn't tell our Doris what Meat Loaf meant in his song, I made a brew and brought my David Baldacci to the armchair.

I must have been sat there half an hour when she piped up with, 'I don't think we'll go to the do this year, 'arold, not when we've got our New Year's party – people might get the impression that we are being frivolous with our retirement fund.'

'We worked hard for that retirement fund, our Doris,' I said. I put the book down and met her eyes – I don't recommend it to the untrained professional, looking our Doris in the eye can result in temporary insanity, blindness and on more than one occasion a telephone book thrown at your head. I said to her, I said, 'Is this about Theo?'

I thought I would flinch, every bone in my body were on edge, steeled against the possible threat of a Yellow Pages when she set down her garland and said, 'I would have liked to have followed the song's example, had one last waltz with my grandson before I get too old and he starts properly courting.'

'He's fourteen.'

She shot a quick Look and said, 'Yes, and you were not much older when you started hanging about the Co-Op after me.'

'Times were different then,' I said, 'we didn't have television and there were something about you that called to me.'

'If you're talking about my breasts I'll spiflicate you, 'arold Copeland,' she said returning to her decoration; there were a hint of a smile there, it were hidden beneath her jowls but it were there all right.

'I tell you what, I'm picking him up from school today, I'll take him to the pub and we can have a chat.'

'You're always taking him to that pub for chats,' she said, 'I'm having to tell the ladies group you're trying to steer him away from drinking by using the Hare and Horse as a deterrent.'

I said to her, I said, 'You keep telling them that and I'll keep buying our Theo bitter shandies – it'll put him right off.'

It were getting on for the last week of school and Angela wanted to finish her Christmas shopping without having to contend with Theo and her husband. With Neil at work, I picked Theo up at the school gates and headed off to the Hare and Horse. They'd done the place out for the holidays. It were bitter cold outside – I'd had to wear the driving gloves our Doris bought me because she wanted her husband to look sporting when he dropped her off at certain events – and the pub had lit the fire.

I don't know what it is but there's something about an open fire crackling behind a grate that reminds you of Christmas. I felt like a schoolboy again with the hope of Saint Nicholas in my chest; I could go to bed and not sleep thinking of what I'd open in the morning, sometimes my Mum would wrap books in brown paper and string.

I went to the bar to order, they'd decorated it with tinsel and had a gold banner emblazoned with 'Merry Christmas' in red. Theo took his coat off and I saw he were wearing the green scarf our Doris had knitted him a few years back.

When I sat down I said to him, I said, 'You've not cast her off completely then?'

He looked at me gone out, like he'd been expecting his Grandad to get a bit senile but he hadn't expected it to happen so soon. He said to me, 'Who're you on about?'

'Your Nan,' I said, 'she wouldn't want you to know but she's a bit sneeped since you've said you won't dance with her at the church hall.'

He said to me, he said, 'It's embarrassing, Grandad. I stopped dancing lessons years ago and I've got exams, I didn't have time to organise a dance with her.'

'Which bit do you want me to tell her?' I were being harsh now, I could tell, but grandsons are a lot easier to blackmail than wives, 'That she embarrasses you or that she's not worth your time?'

I had him there. He didn't say anything, sat there watching the bubbles rise in his shandy and I were reminded of the time I caught him reading the Beano in the back bedroom after our Doris had told him the Beano perpetuated the idea that all young men had to behave as brutes to make friends.

He said to me, he said, 'I don't want to dance with her.'

'Do you want to know what your grandmother is doing right now, Theo? What my wife of fifty-four years has decided to spend the day listening to, with no thought as to what her at number forty-two might say, never mind Mrs Witstanley.'

He shrugged at me, gone out, and said to me, he said, 'What's she doing?'

'Listening to Meat Loaf.'

He looked at me as though I had definitely gone insane. I could see it there in his eyes, it were almost like he were a toddler again and wary of eating anything green. He picked up his drink and scrutinised it, one eye half-shut.

'You haven't had any yet,' I said.

'It could have been fumes,' he said, 'you might have had a few too many sherries at lunch and now you're trying to get me to dance with Nan. Is this all because you want me to dance with Nan? If I come back to yours will I find her writing a letter to the Gazette about the utter lack of unadulterated hummus at the last ladies luncheon?'

I shook my head and said to him, I said, 'She went to Boots and got upset over wrinkle cream.'

And he said, 'It's not wrinkle cream she needs it's re-plastering.'

I struggled to hide the smile behind a stern expression as I said to him, I said, 'That's your grandmother you're talking about and she deserves her last waltz with her grandson.'

'Why?' he said, 'She only does it to show off in front of her friends.'

I said, 'That's her way.'

'Well it's a stupid way,' he said, 'she should stop worrying about impressing people and worry about her family.'

'Would you say that to her face?' I said.

He shook his head. 'No.'

I said to him, I said, 'Then best not saying anything at all, don't you think? We're not having an argument, you've told me why you don't want to dance with her and that's fine, but you need to go to her and explain why.'

He didn't look up from the table as he said, 'Let me finish my shandy first.'

Our Doris had switched the tape to Bon Jovi by the time we returned. She'd moved to her desk in the cubby hole and sat scrawling a letter. Theo walked straight up to her and said, no thought about it, he said, 'Nan we need to talk.'

She capped her pen and sat erect in her seat, her lips pursed and a glint in her eye I know only too well. I should have gone in and stopped Theo from talking, lead him from the house and told him to run because he had raised the ire of our Doris; it were like the devil uncoiling in her stomach – she had more humbug in her face than Scrooge, more anger than the Grinch and she were about to bare it all to Theo. She spoke in clipped tones, as though she were the judge and he were about to be executed, she said to him, she said, 'I don't fear there's much for us to discuss, Theodore, you do not wish to dance with me and even if your grandfather has managed to convince you otherwise there is simply not enough time in which to organise a dance that will be a visual splendour.'

But Theo didn't rise to the bait. I couldn't believe it, he knew what to say to shut her up. He pecked her cheek and with a quick, 'Thanks Nan,' beggared off upstairs to the spare bedroom to get changed.

Our Doris looked deflated again, as though someone had managed to fill her with air but hadn't realised she had a puncture.

I said to her, I said, 'Should I turn the music off?'

She said, 'Touch that dial and I will not be responsible for my actions.' She looked down at the notepaper in her hand and in a few rips tore it to shreds, letting it spill through the air like confetti.

On the twelfth she sent me off to the Hare and Horse whilst she got the vicar in to help her with the decorating. She says as using the vicar gives the place an air of prestige and his help means as the house is truly blessed for the festive period. I think it's because if I go too high up a ladder I get vertigo and I once ruined one of her mother's ornamental shepherds when I fell on him in nineteen-seventy-three.

Alf had a pint on the table when I got there. I sat down and he said to me, 'Merry Christmas from me to thee.'

I knocked back a third of the pint and said to him, I said, 'I think that's the best present you've ever given me, Alfred, must have been a beggar to wrap.'

He smiled at that and said, 'What's this I've been hearing about your Theo not wanting to dance with Doris?'

'How did you hear about that?'

'Haven't you read the Gazette?' he said, his eyes all sneaky, as though he'd managed to successfully pull off his biggest heist of pork pies and liquor.

I said, 'What's she been up to this time?'

Funnily enough Alf had a copy handy – had kept it hidden in the inside pocket of his long jacket. I think his Edith must be happy when winter comes around; it's the only time he leaves the house without the worry of him flashing his bits. He opened the newspaper up like an orator preparing to give his speech, as though he'd just been named town crier and wanted to make a huge job of it. He found a page and folded it over, I knew which page it was immediately, our Doris has been featured there that many times I'd be a fool not to recognise the heading of the letters page.

Alf planted his finger over the title, some pun or other that I didn't understand nor care to read. I was more struck by our Doris's letter; it listed the failings of modern public schools in instilling the fear of the elderly and how perhaps children should be taught to respect their elders. And she mentioned Theo. Not by name but any description of a tall, blonde teenage boy of whom our Doris has shared a mutual interest, would be enough for the gossip-mongering folk of Partridge Mews.

I thought she'd torn up the letter. My heart were in my ears, I were clenching the edge of the table; Theo wouldn't stand for this. He'd be right round at his grandmother's. My hands shook as I picked up my pint, I almost spilled perfectly good ale on the mahogany. I said to Alf, I said, 'She's done this on purpose, thinks it'll force Theo's hand and he'll have to dance with her.'

Alf said, 'Will it work?'

'You've met my family, Alf, there's no bleeding telling what they'll do.'

When I got home our Doris weren't at the door. On the twelfth she's usually waiting for me with a mince pie, expecting a comment on her decorations. She did a good job this year and all, the paper garlands weren't just hung from the ceiling, they were festooned, hundreds of little interlocking chains in primary colours and it looked fantastic. An angel sat on top of the mantelpiece, surrounded by photographs of various family members, transferred into festive frames for the season. Our Doris's parents took pride of place beside the angel, her mother resplendent in her wedding dress. In the left hand corner, behind our Doris's Arighi Bianchi sofa, stood the tree; the vicar would have collected it that morning from the farm just outside town. Fairy lights were strung around the needles but weren't yet twinkling, that'd come at night when we sat with cocoa – our Doris chose the setting months ago, depending on the sort of mood she wished them to convey.

Our Doris doesn't go in for tinsel – ever since Janice Dooley of Little Street was Miss December in the Gadsden and Taylor calendar. She used it to cover up her extremities and our Doris said as it were more to do with the fact that she's a face like she doesn't put enough sugar in her lemon curd.

There were no rock music playing but there were a commotion in the kitchen. Theo glared at our Doris with a look that weren't far from the one I'm used to seeing on his grandmother's face. 'There's a bloody reason I didn't want to dance with you, you old bat, it's because you do things like this.'

Our Doris looked ready to spout forth but caught one look at me and she were the simpering woman, all drooping eyes, as though she were close to a stroke but not yet sure about it. She said to me, she said, 'You heard him, our 'arold, tell him to leave.'

'I'm telling him nothing, our Doris, you've done wrong.' I'd pay for it later. Trying to make our Doris see your way of thinking is reminiscent of throwing yourself against a wall and expecting to pass through. I said to her, I said, 'Theo came back here the other day to say he'd dance with you and you told him you didn't want to – you can't blame the lad for doing as you saw fit.'

For a moment something like shock passed across our Doris's face before she said, 'You did not intimate as to your plans, I cannot be held responsible for your lack of information.' She wandered towards the cubby hole.

Theo followed her and he said to her, 'You still sent the letter, Nan, even though you told me you didn't want to dance you still sent the letter. You can't go around throwing your toys out of the pram when you don't get your own way.'

And she said, 'You can't possibly understand, you are too young to understand the politics of polite society.'

He looked at me and I didn't know what to say. I didn't know what passed through Theo's mind as he said to her, he said, 'Bye,' and walked out and it was as though he were never here, as though I hadn't just walked into the heat of a battle between our Doris and grandson. I've never known two people more alike - he wouldn't invite a lad to his fifth birthday party because he was from Cheadle. And now they'd sworn war against one another.

I looked at our Doris, stubborn in her cubby hole, and for some reason, some unfathomable reason I said, 'Merry Christmas,' and followed Theo out the door.

I wound up wandering around town, my bobble hat pulled down over my ears and a scarf trapping all of the air from my mouth. I don't recommend a walk in the middle of the night in December – especially when you're seventy-four. Some folk would have called my ending up at the Christmas tree a sign from above, all I could think about was the second Home Alone film when that lad ends up foiling burglars in ways that nowadays would earn him an ASBO.

I didn't give too much thought to that film, instead I were thinking about how to get our Doris and Theo back on speaking terms. Neither of them likes to apologise and Theo once went three months without speaking to our Doris when she took his crayons off him for colouring on the walls. Both of them had said they wanted to dance with the other – well Theo said he would which I'd have to take to mean the same thing.

I looked at the scene with Mary and Joseph and did what all those folk in all those films think, if Christmas is a time for miracles then maybe I would be able to get our Doris to apologise and get Theo to dance.

I put the plan into action in the morning, folk had started turning out of the pubs and I didn't fancy getting accosted by a PVC-clad Mrs Claus.

At two o'clock in the afternoon on the thirteenth, I woke up. I felt refreshed, I'd had the best night's sleep I'd had in a long time.

Then I remembered the task that lay ahead.

Theo would be finishing school soon so I needed to put my plan into motion. I didn't bother with a shower – sprayed myself liberally with some Lynx deodorant we save in case Theo has to stay the night – and headed off into town. It took me the best part of half an hour to find what I were looking for. Deciding to buy Christmas cards with less than a fortnight to the big day didn't leave me with much choice and I ended up forking out the better part of ten pounds for a card that was fit for purpose.

Now came the difficult part.

Our Doris has perfected her handwriting over the last seventy-two years so that it is equal parts upper-class as casual. There's a flourish to every word that does not look too sentimental but doesn't look common either. It's how you know you're in her good books is that flourish, and I had to use it now. I wrote the only possible word I could think of that Doris might approve; it weren't much, it weren't as tidy as our Doris's script but it would have to do.

I drove to our Angela's, posting the card through the letterbox without knocking and hoping beyond hope that no one had looked out the window as I'd hobbled down the path, certain my feet were frostbitten.

Ultimately our Doris decided she had to attend the church hall Christmas party. She maintains it were because she had to be seen near Janice Dooley of Little Street, who had been invited, though she isn't a fully-fledged member of the WI, merely in control of the garden safari. Besides, Violet Grey would be there and our Doris would love nothing more than Doug Grey to be found making sinful exclamations to Janice behind the church hall.

Angela, Neil and Theo sat at the same table with Alf and Edith on the table across – Theo and our Doris avoided making eye contact. They'd pass vegetables but they wouldn't share jokes from their crackers and although our Doris bought him a bitter shandy neither of them spoke of it.

I didn't crack my dentures on the vegetables and the turkey tasted like turkey so the dinner turned out all right. The music started midway through and some of the others were up and gliding across the dance floor like spectres of death.

I were just about to dig into my Christmas pudding when she appeared, as though she'd come from the mist like some ghost in a horror film. Violet Grey. She wore a dark purple dress and fake pearls; one must never appear too flush at a church hall Christmas soiree, and she'd had her hair done up in a beehive. She must have thought she looked a bit all right and I thought she looked a bit like something out of Star Trek.

Violet made straight for Theo, standing over him so that she nearly sagged on top of his head. She flickered her eye-lashes like moths against a lampshade and said to him, she said, 'I was most worried to read of a young man choosing not to dance with his grandmother, Theodore, I thought you a much more sensible boy than that.'

Theo straightened his spine and stared Violet straight in the eye and said to her, and this will have made our Doris proud, this will have, he said, and it were the veritable icing on the cake, he said, 'I do so dislike gossip, Mrs Grey. After all, I have no qualms about dancing with my grandmother, quite similar to you having no qualms about the activities Mr Grey and Miss Dooley are getting up to in the Scout Hut.' He stood up and held his hand out to our Doris and said to her, he said, 'Would the lady care for a dance?'

Our Doris were positively beaming as she said, 'I'd like nothing more.'

He led her into the middle of the dance floor as the next song began playing; I'd never have thought you could waltz to Bat out of Hell.

6

SECATEURS

Our Doris teamed up with Alf's Edith to ban us from seeing each other.

It all started after the New Year's party; our Doris weren't happy to discover Alf on the patio surrounded by vol-au-vents with a copy of the Daily Star. If it had been one of my Daily Mirrors it would have been bad enough – I'm still trusting Alf's Edith not to mention anything to our Doris about what's really hidden in the plant pots in my shed. She thinks it's National Geographics, I think she can cope with the idea of pornography for the upper class gentleman but the idea of her husband reading a red top? It ends with me having to pay for the latest expensive gadget to help her in the kitchen.

For our forty-fifth anniversary I bought her an electric tin opener. She'd seen something similar in a Kleeneze catalogue but wouldn't buy it because she thought it catered to the common man and because our Kleeneze woman came from the council estate with a Tesco trolley full of magazines. I think if people didn't see her, our Doris might have rethought matters, but the lass takes two buses to get here and that's too lower class individual for our Doris. I said to her, I said, 'Her produce is the same as Violet Grey's Kleeneze lady.' But she were having none of it.

She said to me, she said, 'Violet Grey does not have a Kleeneze lady. If Violet Grey had a Kleeneze lady then I would know about it. Do you know what I do know, our 'arold? Violet Grey still serves Ringtons lemon wafers at the ladies group. What do I serve, our 'arold? Waitrose custard creams – I might as well be part of the lower classes, swilling the undercarriages of dustbins with a hosepipe.'

I said to her, and I think I must have been feeling a bit fearless, I said, 'You'll have to find one better than ours, our Doris, it's got a leaky spout.'

The Look didn't get a, well it didn't get a look in as she expounded, 'Brilliant, not only am I attempting to clean another wastrel's bins but I'm using a hosepipe with a leaky spout. If I hear that you've told people about our hosepipe, our 'arold, I'll have your guts for garters.'

She's like that is our Doris; uses all the old-fashioned sayings to get her point across, but ask her to wear the same dress twice to an evening do and you'd think you'd committed blasphemy.

So I bought her the electric tin opener.

And she used it once.

Then she donated it to the charity shop because electric tin openers highlighted the laziness of modern society and her donation would help reduce her carbon footprint. I were surprised she didn't take it one step further and write a letter to the Gazette informing them as to how she were taking aims to lead a greener lifestyle.

Back to the New Year's party: as we reached the ten minute countdown, our Doris started to round people up. She's always had an itinerary has our Doris and she were none too pleased that Theo had run amok because her family always have to stand with each other. She doesn't invite her cousin Mavis, so the entirety of the Partridge Mews Women's Institute – plus husbands and significant others – get to witness her family with smiles on their faces watching the fireworks Angela's brother-in-law brings.

But Theo were nowhere to be found. Mrs Sterling said as she had seen him heading out back with Alf, and if that weren't the red rag to the bull I don't know what were. Our Doris's pace picked up – she could have been a marathon brisk walker the way her Hotter sandals scuffed across the lino.

And there she found them. Alf and our Theo, completely off their heads – Theo were that far gone he were practically unconscious. I thought our Doris would scream, I could see the heat rising in her face like she'd just swallowed the sun. She said to me, she said, 'Get Neil to take him upstairs, we'll tell them that Theo's been taken ill – and put that monstrosity in your shed.' She shot an ounce of the Look at Alf and fired off the killer blow, 'I'm going to talk to his Edith.'

And now we're not allowed to see each other.

Our Doris told me the next morning when we were cleaning the kitchen. Someone had squashed quiche into the carpet and hidden it beneath the hearth rug. There's a story behind the rug that involves our Doris at the British Home Stores, bad map-reading skills and cattle; it's memorable; memorable enough that our Doris notices every small kink and bump in the fabric. As I cleaned, she informed me that Alf and I would no longer be allowed to frequent our most popular haunts.

I said to her, I said, 'Everyone gets drunk, our Doris, it'll do Theo some good to know what a hangover feels like.'

She gave me the Look and said to me, she said, 'Underage alcoholism is a perfect pastime for the lower classes, our 'arold, they've got nothing better to do. Our grandson, however, drinks black coffee not White Lightning. If I ever catch Alfred Simpson anywhere near our grandson again, I'll let everyone know just where he hides those pork pies.' With that, our Doris surged to the sink to scour pans whilst I contemplated a life without stolen pork pies and days out to the police station.

This isn't the first time that our Doris has banned me from seeing someone. In the late nineties she thought I was too obsessed with Charlie Dimmock and wouldn't let me watch Ground Force; then she started attending Pandra O'Malley's craft group and I figured out how to utilise my video recorder to its optimum standards. By the time our Doris found out, I had recorded two series, including an episode where she leant over a skip and her green vest slipped forward just enough for me to imagine what was going on underneath. I keep them hidden in the loft, alongside the old television and bring them out when she invites the ladies group over – I use headphones and keep the volume down, she hasn't cottoned on yet, or if she has she doesn't say anything.

Which meant she wouldn't be able to keep us apart for long.

Or so I thought.

I had to wait in for a pair of new secateurs. I'd seen them in the newspaper – recommended by Charlie Dimmock, with an extendable attachment for those hard to reach places. I hadn't told our Doris because she doesn't like the neighbours to think I'm not fit enough to climb ladders and remove foliage with the old rusty pair I had off my father when he died twenty-seven years ago.

I got our Theo to drop a note to Alf using Dave the Tesco security guard as the middle man; they've developed something of a camaraderie over Alf's years of failing to pay for things. It happens that often I think it keeps Dave in work.

Our Doris doesn't use the Tesco in town, has always called it an off-set of bigger supermarkets, designed to combat the laziness of the common overweight mother with Ugg boots and sagging denim crotches with frayed heels.

I think she must have had her suspicions – that all-seeing eye renowned in the field of housewifery must have flared and told her that her husband was up to something. She asked Angela if she would take her into town and, Angela tells me, after she perused every shop from the chalkboard windows of the independent Partridge Mews stores to the sparkling mannequins of the big brand clothing chains, our Doris decided that for the first time in fifteen years – since the fruition of that miniature supermarket – she would take a look at what she described as, 'the affordable prospects of the disenchanted'.

Once inside, she bypassed the aisles and found Dave.

I can see him in my mind's eye reading another Clive Cussler, wondering if his husband has put the chicken in the oven, when our Doris appears. And she has her lips pursed, as though she is Edwina Currie about to deliver the truth about what's really in his Spanish omelette, and she says to him, she says, 'I believe that my grandson may have left some correspondence on your person in the hopes that you would operate as a postman. I understand that impersonating a postman might not be a criminal offense but how do you think your manager would react if he were to find out that instead of apprehending criminals you have been helping them with their own illicit activities.'

Angela says that Dave stared at her dumbfounded and his hands were positively shaking as he handed the note over.

When our Doris returned she had a different kind of smile on her face, the sort that makes you think you'd have better chance facing a python as it crushes you, that as your lungs collapsed you'd have a waft of a Ventolin inhaler and be sorted because Doris's jaw looked fit to unhinge and swallow me in one fell swoop and most folk know that once your wife catches you with that vice-like stare you're done for.

At first I thought it were about my new secateurs. I'd hidden them in the shed in a hollowed out copy of a Collins dictionary, and planned to take them out when she next had her WI meeting, all ready to tell her that Peter had dropped them round because they weren't working for him and he wanted someone to get some use out of them. She's had a soft spot for Peter since she ruined his prize marrow and his wife didn't go to the Gazette.

Then I saw the note. She held the paper in a pincer grip between thumb and forefinger. All air left the room. Our Doris stopped in front of me and said to me, she said, 'Where do you think I've been?'

If my mouth didn't go as dry as the Gobi desert in a heatwave, then my tongue turned to sandpaper. Our Doris gave me The Look and said, 'I had a thought you'd try something like this – but to commandeer a man whose very profession is to keep the peace, it makes me question if you've learned anything over the last fifty years or if it's a repeat of Mrs Turner's Sunday School class and you've just been saying what your Aunty Barbara told you to.' She dropped the note on top of my newspaper and left the room and I knew to be on edge – the hairs on the back of my neck wouldn't lie down and I were that cold I thought I'd end up with hypothermia but she didn't come back into the living room, she decided that it was the perfect time to defrost the freezer on top of the fridge.

The freezer that I'd hidden a packet of smoked mackerel in because I can't stand the stuff.

A packet of smoked mackerel that our Doris defrosted and cooked and fed to me and I spent the rest of the evening picking bones out of my dentures, questioning why mackerel bones had to be that fine as to wriggle into Fixadent.

My plan failed and our Doris wouldn't let me out of her sight. I had to attend the New Year's meeting of the Partridge Mews Women's Institute in which they discussed their upcoming trip to a Mrs Burr's tea room in Wren's Lea – in which they would read Jane Austen to the elderly on the other end of the spectrum; the ones who've lost control of either their bowels, bladder or both – and once that was over they would partake in afternoon tea. Within fifteen minutes I was nodding off, when they got to questioning whether Mrs

Hodgson's magnetic dentures could cope with Rocky Road I were doddering and by the time they reached scarves that would appear modest but professional I were gone entirely, dozing past the tea break. Our Doris didn't wake me until halfway through The Chase by which point I'd missed my chance to shout about people's lack of education when it comes to Hattie Jacques.

The next morning our Doris decided that all meetings with Theo had to be supervised to make sure I didn't attempt to lead him astray, because he might fancy a career in politics one day. I didn't say that if he wanted to then sneaking notes to Alf under our Doris's nose is just the sort of subterfuge you expect from a politician. Instead I said to her, I said, 'I'm going down the allotment, see how that clematis is getting on.'

I'd caught her on a good day – she had plans to meet a reporter from the Partridge Mews Gazette about her place as fifth house in the garden safari; secured, she says because she is a horticulturist visionary with the required prowess to get what she wants. It has nothing to do with the fact that she has intimate knowledge of the lives and loves of every member of the WI and a penchant for claiming her age means she just doesn't know what secrets she'll be able to keep. My talk of the clematis gave her a bit of information she could pass on to make herself look like she knew a thing or two about gardening when in actual fact if dirt so much as touches her French manicure she's bemoaning the fact that we never did that decking in nineteen-eighty-four when Mr Pritchard-Singh had it on special offer at the hardware store.

I were just about to go through the door when she said to me, she said, 'Do try and steer clear of the house until after three o'clock, our 'arold, I won't be able to get the Vax out with the reporter here.'

I nodded and hid a grin beneath a copy of the Telegraph. That gave me seven hours free – seven hours in which I might be able to sneak down to the Hare and Horse and have a few with the lads. When I reached the car I couldn't figure out how to hatch any sort of Alf-related plan. The husbands of Partridge Mews know what's good for them and what's good for them usually involves steering clear of getting involved in thwarting our Doris's schemes.

Which meant I was on my own.

I'd been in the same position before. Our Doris wanted to stop me from attending evening classes at the college – she claimed I wasn't interested in art I just wanted to sneak a glance at Magdalena Valentine's bare form. I said as Magdalena was a captivating subject to draw, not because of her breasts but because of the way certain parts of a fifteen stone woman settle. Either way our Doris won and the lads wouldn't get involved; steered clear of telling their wives that the tutor said as I had a knack for using charcoal. Their continued attendance saw a rise in the amount of male students at the adult learning centre. Meanwhile I stayed home and listened to The Archers; and that took fifty years to get your pulse racing.

I got to the allotment, wondering if Ben would let me borrow his tarpaulin, I thought I might be able to find Alf and smuggle him into my shed; I keep some cans of bitter in old paint tins, we're not dead yet so I don't think they're toxic. But then our Doris had told me to steer clear until three and I'm not sure I could locate him, wrap him up and gain the required strength to lift Alf into the shed in four hours.

I didn't have to ask Ben, he were nowhere to be seen in any case. When I reached my patch, sat in a ratty deck chair with his head hidden under a balaclava, looking like something out of The Bill, was Alf. He said to me, he said, ''ow at, 'arold.' And I said to him, I must have been feeling funny, the thought of a day without Doris filled me with some sort of unbridled enthusiasm for mischief and I said to him, I said, 'Put the chair back in the shed, we're going down the pub.'

He threw the deck chair, slammed the door and practically vaulted over the gate in his haste to find ale. 'You better hurry then, 'arold,' he said, 'if the WI sees us then they'll notify the Führer.'

I said to him, I said, 'Your Edith's not that bad.'

'It's your Doris I'm on about, you must admit she's got a knack.'

I said nothing and we sped off towards the Hare and Horse. Alf kept his balaclava on – kept shovelling pork scratchings beneath the wool, his eyes darting around the pub. I said to him, I said, 'Keep looking that shifty and they'll think you've been on the rob again.'

Alf leant forward and he said to me, more of a whisper than anything. 'Why the bleeding heck do you think I was at your allotment? I'm in need of an alibi, 'arold.'

I've never downed a pint so fast in my life – especially considering our Doris has me on a strict diet of half measures – it were gone that quickly I'd be surprised if they found any alcohol in my bloodstream at all, if it didn't flush itself out immediately like some sort of express train through my liver.

I said to him, I said, 'We're meant to be coming up with ways to get our wives to let us see each other and you go back to Tesco. I'll have to speak to Dave, see if

I can't get him to let go of this one – claim senility again, it worked at the Co-Op.'

'That were because the manager were too busy trying to hide the fact he kept Jack Daniels in his office drawer – remember it were in the Gazette?' Alf shrugged and said to me, he said, 'Besides, this weren't at Tesco – you can't really call it stealing – not with it being a charity shop, they'll never know.'

'You stole from a charity shop? Your grandson works at a charity shop.'

'They were letting me have them, said that they'd been on the shelf for a while and would I like them as a New Year's gift, only the area manager's caught on – saw me take them and they can't admit they gave them away otherwise they'll lose their jobs. Our Martin's having to deny he knows me.'

'Is this the same area manager who was caught topless on the dual carriageway?'

Alf nodded. 'She says as the underwire in her bra had become potentially life-threatening and that it had to be removed.'

'And now she's got the police after you?'

'I couldn't hide with the old folk because they've started keeping a register. I mean they can't remember their names half the time, but their bleeding carers can. One of them said to me, and she's in a high-vis jacket, she said that she could tell I didn't have dementia because I could dribble on cue and she'd seen me give directions to Queen's Street without having to consult an A to Z, I mean, I ask you – she could have earned a bit more cash for keeping quiet instead she tells me to look at a career in amateur dramatics. It makes you wonder just what the world's coming to when you can't trust your local community care workers doesn't it?'

I ordered another pint as Linda went past and said to Alf, I said, 'Are the police after thee or not, Alfred Simpson?'

'Don't use my full name, 'arold', my mother used to use my full name and it still gives me flashbacks to when she'd get the slipper out.

'Much use that bleeding did – you've got the police after you for stealing from a charity shop. It's a charity shop, Alf, not a supermarket, the police aren't just going to let you off with a caution.'

He dropped his head in his hands and he said to me, he were wailing at this point, 'I know, I know, it's all my fault. If this gets around to my Edith she'll have me strung up. She's a pillar of the community – she's a volunteer – she'll have me sleeping in the car, and you know how my bones get in the cold. I'll have to get myself imprisoned – do you think they give protection to criminals?'

I didn't say anything but looked around the pub – Derek O'Malley were there and he would ring his wife quicker than anything because he's looking to a Mediterranean cruise next year and wouldn't fancy his chances if he were harbouring any criminals or knew of their whereabouts. Linda brought my drink and said to me, she said, 'I've heard Yvonne Stephens in the back and she says as she's just rung your Angela to let her know where you are. I'd scarper if I were you, 'arold.'

I handed her the cash and said to her, I said, 'Thanks Linda, you have the drink, I don't want to be over the limit.'

'I'll ring you a taxi, you can pick the car up later.'

I said to her, and I don't know why I did it, I said, 'Tell them we're going down to the police station. Alf has some explaining to do.'

On the way I said to Alf, 'If you hand yourself in they'll think more of you – might give you a bit of leniency when it comes to sentencing.'

He'd removed the balaclava by now, had it rung between his hands like a noose and he said to me, he said, 'I wouldn't be getting sentenced if it weren't for you, 'arold, I could have gone on the run.'

'The only way you're getting out of this is by running into the middle of the road, Alf, your hip's about as much use as Hovis to a coeliac.'

It didn't take long to get to the police station - it's a big concrete block of a building, as though the builders had some stock left over and thought a great grey monolith was imposing enough to stop any level of criminal activity in the town. The reception desk has had that much leftover sticky tack stuck to it that it looks as though someone got bored enough to shoot spitballs at the woodworm.

Geoff Pollock were there, and he said to me, he said, 'You've heard then, Mr Copeland?'

I looked at Alf and said, 'How many people know? I thought he'd only just done it.'

'He?'

I nodded at Alf and said, 'He stole from the charity shop, hasn't told me what he took like but it must be bad if folk are talking about it.'

Geoff's hands had no idea what to do, they flittered through paperwork like moths underneath curtains and he said to me, he said, 'The area manager called and said she'd made a mistake – her staff told her he'd been taking CDs to the skip and she'd got the wrong end of the stick, very reasonable about it she was as well. We rang Mrs Simpson about half an hour ago.'

'Then what have I heard?'

'I had to ring your Angela because we couldn't get hold of you.'

I didn't know whether it were the pint but I had to hold onto the desk. I hadn't felt so funny since Andrea Hayes removed her stockings to show me her scab at the back of the Easter service in nineteen-forty-seven. I said to Geoff, I said, 'Our Doris told me to stay out until three o'clock because she had a reporter from the Gazette going around.'

Geoff nodded and said to us, he said, 'It seems she and the reporter had a bit of a disagreement – he doesn't want to press charges but we're still going to have to let her off with a caution, Mr Copeland, you can't just go around beating reporters with secateurs.'

'She did what?' I knew I'd raised my voice – my ear drums could have popped with the noise, burst like land mines as I envisaged our Doris taking my new secateurs towards the reporter. 'You've not taken them as evidence, have you, I only got them out of the catalogue last week – recommended by Charlie Dimmock – cost me an arm and a leg.' A door opened and our Doris were led out wearing her beige M&S mac, the one she says isn't fit for special occasions but is quite capable of keeping you inconspicuous when you don't want to be seen. And I said to her, yelling across the reception, I said, 'What were you doing with my new secateurs, our Doris?'

She tried for a Look and said to me, she said, 'Don't you raise your voice to me, 'arold Copeland, not when you've got that scruff with you, you've no idea what I've been through.'

'Who're you calling the scruff?'

'You attacked a reporter, our Doris, unless he were making attempts on your life I'm going to find it difficult to understand what you think you were doing with my new secateurs.'

'If you must know, our 'arold, it wasn't about the fifth house at all but about whether I could shed any light on the recent news.'

'What news?' Alf were sat down reading an old Woman's Weekly at this point and I thought that just goes to show the state of our friendship when he won't even support me when my wife is trying to explain her crimes.

'Janice Dooley of Little Street has revealed that she is the mother of Mr Gadsden's long lost lovechild and he has returned to stake a claim in the business. I tell you, that woman will do anything to keep me out of the spotlight.' And with that our Doris swept from the police station, leaving me to collect her things.

I suppose our Doris had used the secateurs properly, only I'd planned on keeping back Japanese knotweed rather than reporters of the Partridge Mews Gazette.

7

EXTRA-MARITAL

Our Doris has been removed from the garden safari.

She received the letter this morning when she were eating her poached eggs. I thought she'd choked on a shell, her throat closed up and her eyes squinted and her lips were screwed up that tight they'd have done a good job keeping the Tower of London locked. Her face were nearing on beetroot when she wailed like a banshee and said to me, she screamed, 'Who does Janice Dooley think she is? Her biggest claim to fame is that she can still walk after spending all that time on her back. If she hadn't been sleeping with Doug Grey then she would never have been given the garden safari. I should have listened to my mother – she told me to meet someone with money in his pocket and what did I do? I married for love. Love? It was the nineteen sixties – I could have been Paul McCartney's bit on the side – could have put aside my differences and set foot in Liverpool but no, I married a man who thought to hide a pair of secateurs in the Collins English Dictionary!'

I thought it probably weren't best to take another bite of my toast – thought the crunch might make the silence that bit more awkward than it already were and I said to her, I said, 'I don't think the dictionary had anything to do with it, our Doris. You still would've attacked that journalist.'

'He wasn't a journalist – he were the only person at the Gazette who had paper in his notepad and a fully functioning pencil. And I only beat him with the secateurs, it's not like I used them to chop off his threepenny bits.' She folded the letter up and set it back in the envelope – her nose scrunched up then, her eyes seemed to roll back in her head and she sniffed the air as though she were testing for gas.

I said to her, I said, 'What's up, our Doris?'

She held up her hand and shushed me before she lifted the envelope up to her nose and sniffed along the edge of the torn paper. Our Doris went straight to the Look and said to me, she said, 'You'll never guess what that lemon tart has gone and done, our 'arold, at least when I spray scent on my correspondence it's nothing as cheap as Dove's cucumber anti-perspirant.' And our Doris did something I never thought she would do, she flung the envelope across the room and watched it sail right into the Poundstretcher plant pot her Mavis bought me as a Christmas present.

I did something I never thought I'd do; it could have been equal parts heroic and incredibly stupid. I creaked my chair back so it made that sound that goes through you like olive oil and I retrieved the letter. It definitely had some funny scent about it – it prickled at your nostrils, like hay when me and our Doris used to go and frolic in Mr Sterling's fields; it were the sixties and we couldn't always afford the flicks. I fetched the letter back to my seat and read it aloud, it read, 'Dear Mrs Copeland, after much deliberation the committee has decided that unfortunately we are going to have to remove your house from the garden safari due to its association with you and the recent scandal surrounding your name, sincerely yours Ms. Janice Dooley.' I shook my head and said to our Doris, I said, 'She's got some cheek, hasn't she – she's created enough scandal herself.'

Our Doris looked me dead straight in the eye then like Clint Eastwood in the final showdown and she said to me, she said, 'There is no scandal – there's no lovechild, 'arold, Janice Dooley finally has the chance to build something of a career for herself. It was intimated to me by none other than Pandra O'Malley that Janice thinks she can make it onto one of these reality shows – she's in talks with a prominent production company to record a pilot episode of Little Street goes Large. Apparently she'll be front page news in the Partridge Mews Gazette.'

I knew my jaw had dropped, my dentures were practically on my lap. I said to our Doris, I said, 'You'll have to tell someone, our Doris.'

She set her shoulders back and placed her hands demurely on the table before fixing one eye with the Look and she said to me, she replied, 'We do not stoop to the level of a certain Miss Dooley. One does not need to make one's intentions public in order to fuel the fire. I have a meeting with the only other person in this town capable of informing folk of the truth in the correct fashion.'

If my jaw were going to drop any more it'd be around my ankles. I shook my head, convinced that I would have something of a heart attack, or stroke, or one of those things that stops me from enjoying vanilla slices and I said to her, I said, 'You don't mean her.' I choked out the last word, I couldn't speak the name, as though the monster would rise like Beetlejuice if the name were said enough.

And our Doris nodded once, a curt offering, her face practically trembling because we knew what this meant and she said to me, our Doris said, 'Violet Grey will arrive at half past twelve for a light lunch of a chicken salad with new potatoes.'

No doubt I'd be sent off down to the pub and I thought the pint was well-needed. If our Doris and Violet Grey were teaming up with one another then Janice Dooley of Little Street would have hell to pay.

When Violet arrived I knew the situation must be more serious than I thought. She showed up in a taxi with a briefcase in one hand, carrying two coffees in a polystyrene cup holder from Starbucks. She were dressed like Clare Balding in a beige two-piece suit; feminine but she could have knocked out a horse at ten paces. When I greeted her at the door, she said to me, eye-lashes fluttering, smelling like the lavender air freshener our Doris uses on the bins, she said, 'Good morning, Harold, it is a rather sombre moment when we must meet under such unfortunate and distressing circumstances as these.'

Our Doris had dressed for the occasion. She appeared at the kitchen door in a mauve dress with the Bon Marche cardigan she says gives just the air of melancholy required in serious situations – when Nigel fell off that roof in the Archers I thought she'd forever be an apparition in cream wool. In the jewellery department she had settled for her false pearl earrings and the gold chain around her throat I bought for her forty-third birthday. 'Violet, I'm so glad you came, I don't know what I would do without you.' From the look she gave Violet I'm surprised she weren't up for an Oscar. She gave this look through the door of the living room, and it were a look unlike I've ever seen before, it were sad but there was a determined set in her shoulders and as her right hand reached out for the door jamb she gave this hollow stare at herself in the mirror and in that moment I thought, you've been married for nigh on half a century, Harold and you never knew your wife could do this. She owned the stage as she approached us, making wistful looks at the photos of Angela and Theo and assorted family members across the walls.

She reached Violet and I was suddenly furniture, the briefcase and coffees ended up in my hands like I were nothing more than a hat stand. And Violet took our Doris's hands in hers and she said to her, she said, 'Don't you worry about this, Doris, we've dealt with worse things. Remember when Manuela Esperanza wanted to open a tapas bar in the town centre – where did she wind up? Wren's Lea. Some think I was wrong in offering Janice Dooley the place as head of the garden safari – after all, she is not part of the Partridge Mews Women's Institute, some might think her unfit for the position if words are spoken in the correct places.' From the look Violet Grey gave me at that point I knew exactly what I were part of – they were setting the scene, making me a part of their underhandedness.

I, Harold Copeland, had been drawn in to see this. Like children on a playground when someone wore the wrong day's underwear, the ladies of Partridge Mews would be forced to turn on Janice or face the wrath of our Doris. I've been married to her for a long time, and I love her, but when someone crosses her it's like watching a nuclear explosion when you're nothing more than a cockroach.

Our Doris looked at me, her eyes not even fully open. She shook her head like she were trying to get hair out of her eyes – hair that's impossible to get in her eyes, the amount of Silvakrin she uses – and she said to me, she said, 'I think it best if you make yourself scarce, dear, I wouldn't want you to hear anything you shouldn't.'

Violet pretended that she had forgotten I was there and suddenly I were ousted from the house, coat and wallet thrust into my arms, without our Doris questioning what I looked like and I thought to myself, I thought, she's done it on purpose, wants folk to think as she's too upset to focus on the fact her husband is out wearing his brown brogues with his navy trousers.

I went to the only place I could think of in these situations. The Hare and Horse. When I arrived, I ended up waiting for twenty minutes before the doors opened. Alf arrived about quarter of an hour into my first half and came down and sat down without a drink in front of him, an expectant look on his face. He said to me, he said, 'You know I'd have thought your Doris would have stopped you drinking and driving – it's not in fashion nowadays, 'arold.'

I opened my wallet and handed him a tenner saying to him, I said, 'When our Doris has Violet bleeding Grey around our house discussing war tactics, I think I'm owed a bitter.'

And Alf said to me, he said, 'Things must be getting bad if you're willing to throw away a tenner just to get me off your back.'

When he were stood at the bar I started to feel meddlesome and I shouted across the pub, I said, 'Alf, mine's a pint – I'll walk home.' If our Doris wanted folk to think we were in a bit of a disarray what better way to show them – I wouldn't get drunk. I'd get a bit merry, maybe go as far as not knowing which way my legs were turning, and I'd go at home.

Alf put the pint down in front of me as I finished with the half. 'You're working through them a bit quickly aren't you?'

'All I can say to thee, Alf, is that Janice Dooley would be better off doing a midnight flit. Our Doris isn't happy that she stole her thunder – you know she were trying hard for fifth house – and well, it didn't do Janice any favours when she went and did that photo shoot at Tatton Park wearing nothing but a fur coat.' I gulped back the pint, barely noticing the flavour until it were gone.

'Aye, that caused a right stir at the Quiz Night, I can tell thee – some of the young 'uns had her photos on the dart board.' Alf shuddered as though someone had electrocuted his spine and said to me, he said, 'The sight of her neck line were enough to put you off your pork scratchings – I know our Edith isn't happy. She said it would have been all well and good if she'd done it for charity, or tastefully, but wearing her grandmother's fur coat. Did you know she wore that when women won the vote? Our Edith were beside herself when she got the newspaper clippings up on our Martin's computer.'

'Our Doris says as she's going for a television show.' Alf shook his head. 'Don't believe any of it, 'arold. I've had it off Wilkie Pointer himself – Janice has been telling all those that'll listen at the Harrington that the only person she's spoken to is someone from an agency.'

I sat bolt upright in my seat, I went that fast I thought I must have cured my sciatica. I said to Alf, I said, 'What agency?'

'It could've been a letting agency for all I know. I'm sure you'll read all about it in the Gazette this week, when she and the long lost lovechild of Mr Gadsden have their interview. She's a hot topic is Janice Dooley of Little Street – really milking her fifteen minutes of fame. I tell you, 'arold, it'll all come to nothing.'

But he needn't have said anything. All plans for getting merry went out of my head but I still walked home. Alf were going off to the allotments to see if he could score any carrots off Richard Peg – he's got a lot left over now his Dorothea has gone off to the glue factory in the sky – and I set about walking home.

Back in the sixties, when all the trouble first started between our Doris and Janice, everyone thought something must have happened in those months when Janice disappeared. I remember my Mum thinking it were something to do with Janice keeping her head in the sand for the sake of her mother. Cynthia Dooley of Little Street was a figurehead in Partridge Mews – a matriarch – proper Ena Sharples type character, she once had a slanging match with my mother that lasted for twenty minutes during an air raid. Apparently she hadn't returned one of Cynthia's hot water bottles and that would have been fine had her aunty in New Zealand not just dropped dead in a motorbike accident and she were sure it were a sign from the good lord himself that she should see as her hot water bottle were returned. Either way, hot water bottle was given back and no more were said about it.

Well, her blood pressure must have constantly been simmering in her veins because in nineteen-fifty she had a heart attack and after that were warned she shouldn't ever get too hot under the collar, otherwise she might kill herself – her heart did stop in the end, but that were due to the fact she choked on a mint imperial doing the ironing; my mother maintained it were an excellent way to go as it proved that Cynthia were a proper housewife, determined to keep her house tidy even in the throes of death.

Her high blood pressure had everyone worried and that's why we all assumed Janice Dooley had been shipped off for a few months. There'd never been a sign of any lovechild before. Mr Gadsden himself only died a few months back – mid-nineties and still able to fasten his shoelaces – and the recent arrival of a possible heir would question on who'd take control of the factory. If Janice Dooley did have a child then I don't know why she'd keep him a secret for nearly fifty years, she were the first one to brag about paper knickers on the Number 38 to Crewe.

I'd hung onto a bit of information and as I wandered through the front door it stood fixed in my head as something I had to tell our Doris because as much as I didn't want to see Janice Dooley victim of a witch hunt, I didn't want to see my wife lose her place of fifth house after we'd gone through so much to achieve it.

Our Doris sat at the kitchen table. Her head were in her hands – she looked up at me and I can tell this weren't acting, there were still fight there but it were hidden very far beneath the bundles of that Bon Marche cardie. I sat down and I said to her, I said, 'I've heard something I think you need to hear.'

She looked up at me and said, 'It better be more than Violet Grey has to offer – apparently Janice Dooley has said that if anything goes wrong she will reveal that she has been having an affair with Doug for the last twenty years.'

I nodded and I were excited – my heart were going ten to the dozen, I thought I had wild horses in my veins, I questioned whether it could have been the bitter, if it had reached my chest and I were about to slump over on the table we spent the best part of three months looking for. I said to our Doris, there were fire in my blood and I said to her, I said, 'Janice Dooley has been speaking to an agency.'

Our Doris mumbled then, and she never mumbles, has been known to enunciate even when cursed with tonsillitis. She said, 'About the reality show, I know.'

I said to her, 'Could it be an escort agency?'

Our Doris's head turned as though it were a periscope and she said to me, she said, 'Go on, 'arold, you must have more than that.'

I nodded and I were on a roll then, my thoughts were tumbling out like milk onto cereal, I said, 'Mr Gadsden died a few months ago, leaving no conceivable heir but a considerable amount of the company to one of his associates. If an heir came along surely they would be entitled to some of the money. Janice Dooley disappeared but she's always talked about birth control – remember she volunteered to give talks to the old folks about contraception? She's been handed the garden safari –'

'And being friends with the Greys would show that she was still part of the social circle that included Mr Gadsden, even though their affair came out all those years ago, meaning there was every chance that she could have had a child and for whatever reason she and Mr Gadsden hushed it up.' Our Doris flung herself to her feet, chair slamming to the floor, the triumphant gleam in her eyes.

And as soon as it appeared, it vanished. She picked up her chair. 'Now we need proof. We need to get into Little Street.'

The envelope were still on the table between the cruets. I picked it up and wafted it in front of our Doris's face.

'Keep that away from me, our 'arold, you know I can't cope with the smell.'

I said, 'She left you a letter, our Doris, it's practically an invitation to talk. We have our way in.'

Our Doris grinned like the Cheshire Cat on speed and said to me, she said, ''arold Copeland, I knew there were a reason I married for love.'

'I know what it was, it were me dashing good looks.'

The smile slipped slightly, as she nodded, her eyes searching for somewhere else to work. 'Yes, I suppose that must have accounted for something.'

Little Street is a den of iniquity. There's an off-licence on the corner that will serve under-eighteens as long as they're not wearing the school uniform, and everyone seems to own a pitbull. It's one of those streets. I know I've been married to our Doris for a while – some might think that's turned me into a bit of a snob, might have me questioning my sensibilities, might say that this is the world I came from, and they'd be wrong. I might have worn hand-me-downs to school, and my mother might have enjoyed a pint of stout every now and then, but never, would she ever have let her doorstep get as filthy as some of the steps you find down Little Street. They're practically black. I know there've been government cuts but that doesn't mean you can't get out the hot water and a bit of Jeyes Fluid.

I pulled up right outside Janice Dooley's, worried for the safety of my tyres. I have to say I have never been more astonished by a house and that includes the time I saw a shanty town on Comic Relief.

If Cynthia Dooley were alive today she'd have a heart attack. She'd be dead. She'd take one look at the house and that'd be it, she'd be passed out in the gutter, amongst the empty Carlsberg cans and what looked like the remnants of a kebab. All the paint on the front door had chipped, the letterbox had been boarded over, the net curtains were nicotine stained and there were dog-ends of cigarettes all over the front step. I thought something I never thought I'd think – it crossed my mind and I latched onto it like a fly to dog muck – me and Doris were the lucky ones. I said to our Doris, I said, 'Are you sure you can go in there, our Doris?'

She waved her white cotton gloves in my face and said to me, she said, ''arold, I once went into a loft that hadn't been looked at in over twenty years, there were thirty dead bats, a mummified parakeet and the remains of several of Maeve Binchy's early works. I am trained in the art of tact.' And with that she stepped up to the front door.

After three sharp raps the door opened to reveal Janice Dooley bedecked in nothing more than a nylon kimono with egg yolk stains all over the chest. When she saw our Doris this look crossed her face, something between confusion, glee and constipation and she said to us, using this false tone as though she'd swallowed fabric conditioner, she said, 'I cannot say I'm surprised by you're coming here, but I have to say I won't be swayed from my position. I, and a few select members of the group –'

'Committee,' our Doris said, 'and I quite understand your position, Janice –'

'Miss Dooley.'

Our Doris nodded then and inclined her head to the right and if I'd ever seen more of a Look on her I'd have been concussed. She said to Janice, she said, 'Miss Dooley, I understand your position as do so many others across Partridge Mews – you must have seen more ceilings than half the plasterers in town, may we come in?'

Janice's face had practically turned to aubergine and she said to our Doris, opening the door a bit wider, she said, 'You must be upset, Mrs Copeland, do come in.' The first thing I noticed were the smell, she definitely liked her Dove antiperspirant did Janice Dooley, but there were undertones of tobacco, ale, and musk as though the windows hadn't been opened since nineteen-eighty-four. She lead us into the sitting room – an armchair by the window were covered in newspapers and there were the makings of a sandwich on top of the television. I chose a dining chair as our Doris perched on the edge of one of the chairs that sagged more than Ann Widdecombe's jowls and Janice piped up with, she said, 'I'll just go and get changed into something decent.'

Our Doris offered a simpering gaze and said to her, she said, 'If you've not found anything in the last seventy years it's probably best to stop looking.'

Janice nodded and headed off upstairs.

I said to our Doris, I said, 'It's a bit of a rum place

isn't it? I don't remember it being like this when Cynthia had hold of it.'

But our Doris were on her feet again. She said to me, she said, 'We have less than five minutes to find evidence of an escort agency, 'arold, I don't plan on discussing what's gone on in this house in the last half a century.'

I beggared off to the adjoining kitchen whilst our Doris fiddled in the sitting room. I should have been prepared but I'm not sure trained Marines could've entered that kitchen without having to step back and take a breath. There were this odour of pork left too long in the sun – greasy pans filled the sink, egg shells and banana peels and crisp packets spilled out of the bin onto the cracked tiles. If Kim and Aggie were in there they'd find enough microbes on the counter to quarantine the kitchen – it were awful, but it suited Janice Dooley right down to the words on her novelty wine bottle holder, 'one more glass of red and those pots'll be forgotten', complete with scrawled woman.

I weren't too focused on the kitchen if I'm being honest, instead my eyes were on the fridge. A bare-chested, muscular man – they must have been airbrushed, I were fit when I were younger but this fella were built like a Ken Doll, I doubt he'd ever seen a hamburger – he were the main focus on a flyer for an escort agency. The phone number had been circled in black biro and a name written on top surrounded by hearts – Calvin – if Janice Dooley of Little Street were after him he'd need the bleeding muscles. I called through the door to our Doris, I said, 'Come have a look at this, our Doris.'

She were like a bloodhound in that kitchen. The Look didn't cross her face, instead she smirked and got her phone out of her handbag. As she snapped a few pictures on her camera, she said to me, she said, 'If you've proved anything to me today, our 'arold, then it's that there's a reason I married you.'

And then the voice sneered behind us, one of those voices that makes your hairs stand on hair and you shrivel in on yourself, and Janice Dooley said to us, she said, 'If you wished for the name of my kitchen fitter, you could have just asked.' She'd changed into a white blouse and grey pencil skirt, her hair tied up in a bun that revealed how much of her greying hair were really missing.

Our Doris stared at Janice with a look of utter vehemence. Honestly, I thought it might have stripped the wallpaper it were that fiery and she said to Janice, she said to her, 'Which scrap yard do you use? I've never seen this class of corrugated steel in a kitchen before.'

'I had a man put it in for me. I thought you came about the garden safari.'

Our Doris pursed her lips and returned phone to handbag, she said, 'I do – I believe that you have made nothing short of a mockery of the garden safari and are taking the opportunity to further what can only be a rather abysmal career.'

'I'll have you know I was Ms December in the Gadsden and Taylor Calendar.'

'In 1972 – and if there's anything I've learned from this garden safari it's when a flower needs pruning and your petals drooped a long time ago.' Our Doris stepped past Janice and I followed her towards the front door. As we left she turned back and said to her, she said, 'Thank you for the hospitality, Ms Dooley, your home is nothing short of an experience –

something like a Tracey Emin installation, minus the artistic integrity of course.' And with a firm click of the door, our Doris let herself into the street, head held high and said to me, she said, 'Now, 'arold, I think it's time I spoke to the editor of the Partridge Mews Gazette.'

Next week, the Gazette reported of how Janice Dooley of Little Street had hired an escort in order to try and con Gadsden and Taylor with a fake heir. Our Doris carted me down to the church hall to listen to Janice's statement about the goings-on. It looked as though the entirety of Partridge Mews had travelled to the church hall – no wonder our Doris had us arrive an hour early.

Janice Dooley stood at the podium in a tweed two-piece, a few sizes too large for her, and she addressed us all with something just short of a stutter, she said, 'It is with great regret that I must inform you of my intention to step down as head of the garden safari. A position I only received due to the forethought of Mrs Violet Grey, the former head, who has kindly agreed to take back the reins and –' Janice stopped mid-sentence and glared down at our Doris who returned the look with what could only be described as supercilious and she exclaimed, Janice practically screamed, 'beggar this, the whole reason I were given this position were because Violet Grey wanted me to keep Doris Copeland in her place and chose me because I've been having an affair with Doug Grey since nineteen-eighty-three.'

You could have heard a pin drop in the room as Janice stormed off stage and pushed her way through the crowd, but she were held at bay. I watched her go, not noticing that our Doris had risen from her seat and ascended to the podium until she offered a polite cough into the microphone. The hall turned back as our Doris said to them, she said, 'I am sure we can all understand Miss Dooley's pain at losing such a prestigious position due to her wrong-doing. It is often the stress of these situations that makes one resort to such drastic measures. I, myself, made a slight faux pas when it came to a reporter from the Partridge Mews Gazette but we must remember that all publicity, however good or bad, is publicity for the garden safari. Miss Dooley might believe that drawing the attention to such an upstanding member of our community as Doug Grey will lessen the harsh state of her actions, however we mustn't forget that it is only recently she tried something similar against the good memory of Mr Gadsden who many of us will remember as a great friend and confidant. You will all join me in wishing Miss Dooley all the best in the future, and pray that she considers the consequences of her actions, after all who are we if not a forgiving community?'

A thunderous applause greeted our Doris as Janice Dooley raged further and surged through the door of the church hall. I looked up at our Doris in all her glory and felt something like fear, but at that moment, I couldn't have been prouder. She'd done what our Doris does best, she'd won this round.

8

QUINOA

Our Doris has put us both on diets since the Women's Institute decided to reinstate her as fifth house in the garden safari. One Wednesday I woke up thinking I were suffocating when one of my socks were unceremoniously thrown across my face; I thought that was it, after seventy-four years on the planet, my heart had finally given out and there were no air left in my body. Then her dulcet tones rang out across the bedroom, she said to me, she said, 'Hurry up, our 'arold, I want to get weighed before anyone else arrives – you never know the sort of information people'll listen out for once you're on those scales.'

I said to her, thinking I'd croak, I said, 'I can't breathe properly, our Doris.'

'Well take your sock off your chin and stick it on your feet – I went with the thin cotton ones, they'll weigh less.'

I were struggling then, had no idea what she were talking about, and I said to her, I said, 'What's all this talk about weighing for?'

She said to me, she said, 'We're going to try the new slimming club down the church hall. I saw the advert at the last WI. Of course, I don't need to lose much weight, having always been of a slim build, but I think that if I lost a few pounds it might show those less fortunate that even those of us with healthy lifestyles still must put in the work, don't you?'

That's when my trousers were dropped over my waist and I sunk back into the pillows. I thought that it were just my luck, that were, finally on my way – all prepared to head onto wherever you end up and I find out that for me it's Bulge Busters. I pulled the sock off my face and looked at our Doris – the rain were thundering down outside and she were dressed in a pastel pink and cream summer dress she'd bought for the last fête up at Greenfield. I said to her, I said, 'Why don't we just forego the slimming club and I'll pay for thee to have a gastric band?'

She shot a Look my way then and said to me, she said, 'Are you saying that I require gastric surgery in order to lose weight? Do I look like I don't have the presence of mind to watch what I eat? I were born during the war, our 'arold, I have seen rations far worse than nouvelle cuisine, I'm sure that I can cope with carrot sticks and a baked potato.'

'I best get dressed then, hadn't I?' I said, and hobbled off into the bathroom, wondering if they'd subtract the weight of my new knee.

We arrived at the church hall half an hour early to find a young lass bearing a cardboard cut-out of a thin woman with a smile on her face and a tape measure around her waist. A speech bubble had been scribbled around her mouth, 'I couldn't ride a rollercoaster until I joined Bulge Busters.' I said to our Doris, I said, 'That'll be all right then, our Doris, join Bulge Busters and get a free pass to Alton Towers.'

Our Doris gave me the Look and said to me, she said, 'You know fair well that poor individual was too large for a rollercoaster, but due to her sheer determination she has managed to become a model citizen.'

'You always know how to suck the fun out of everything, our Doris,' I said.

''arold, I am sure that the day you say something humorous I will undoubtedly acknowledge the fact, but right now I must endeavour into the church hall so that I may express that if one works hard then one can have the body they always dreamed of.'

I said to her, I said, 'I've been dreaming of Charlie Dimmock but I don't quite fancy having her body.'

She didn't answer me. Instead, she flung open the passenger door and raised herself as though she were Dracula from the coffin and she scuttled towards the young woman, handbag held in the crease of her elbow. She offered that smile of hers, sweet, but with no hint of teeth – that way no one could see she could eat them alive – and she said to the leader, reading the name of her badge, she said, 'Jenny, I presume,' here she extended her hand, as though she were the queen, she'd taken off her cotton gloves and now held them in her left hand as she crossed palms, 'a pleasure to meet you, I must say. I am Mrs Copeland, and this is my husband, Harold. As you will probably have heard, I will be taking part in the Partridge Mews Women's Institute's garden safari as fifth house. I have chosen to join your weight loss program in the hopes of losing a few pounds so as I may inspire other women across the county that with the right strength and determination they might improve their character.'

I shrugged and said to Jenny, I said, 'I'm here for the rollercoaster.'

Jenny didn't smile, the lapels of her blazer seemed to be quaking and she said to us, all false eye-lashes and grins, she said, 'The pleasure is all mine, Mrs Copeland, do come in and make yourself at home. At the moment, as it is your first week, this session will be free but every subsequent class has a charge of seven pounds.'

Our Doris's shoulders were set back as though she were a tank about to take down a small village and she said to her, she said, 'Now Jenny, perhaps you weren't fully aware of the current state of affairs. As I am offering you publicity for your little club, I expected the fee to be waived – of course you may charge my husband however you see fit.'

Jenny picked up two cards and handed them to me. She said to me, she said, 'These are your registration forms, Mr Copeland,' and turning to our Doris she said, 'I have classes throughout Cheshire, Mrs Copeland, it is more than a little club.'

'Oh, I don't doubt that you're quite good at your job, dear, but really as a career path it is little more than whimsy. If you wanted to scorn people for what makes them feel good you should have become a vicar, now where do I weigh?'

Jenny inhaled deep, as though she were in the midst of an asthma attack and she said to our Doris, she said, 'Right this way, Mrs Copeland. You can also make a direct debit through the Bulge Busters website that will go out of the bank on the first of each month for a fraction of the cost.'

'I'm sure that will be a much more suitable option for Harold, if you bring us the forms, our grandson is quite capable with anything relating to computers.' She eyed up the scales like she does fruit at the greengrocers – they were a block on the ground, like something you'd weight cattle on and she said, 'Should I remove my shoes?'

The way Jenny rolled her eyes I was surprised they didn't get stuck in the back of her head and she said to our Doris, she said, 'If you so wish, Mrs Copeland, though they do not need to lose any weight themselves, I imagine.'

Our Doris's eyes intimated that she might swallow Jenny whole. They became practically all pupil. She slipped out of her shoes and stepped onto the scales. I held my breath. It felt like the longest breath I'd ever held. Our Doris glared at Jenny as though her stare would reduce her to ashes.

Finally the scales beeped and our Doris stepped down.

Jenny made a note on her card and picked up a laminated BMI chart. She said to our Doris, she said, 'And how tall do you believe you are, Mrs Copeland, I'd imagine you're about five foot two – one?'

'I am five foot five but how that relates to my weight I do not know.'

'It helps me to calculate your BMI and according to this chart you're currently sixteen pounds above your healthy weight.' I don't think anything would have wiped the glee from Jenny's face. She spoke with such a smile I was almost blinded by the sun shining off her teeth. 'It often happens in older ladies – as your life becomes more sedentary the pounds slip around your waist. Mr Copeland, if you'll step onto the scales please.'

I stepped onto the scales before our Doris could fling them at Jenny. We waited for the beep and I prayed that I was morbidly obese, that Jenny would tell me that at my current weight I should have died in two-thousand-and-five during an episode of Taggart. Instead once the scales beeped, Jenny said to me, she said, 'According to this chart, Mr Copeland, you're of a perfectly healthy weight. If you wish to support your wife in her weight loss journey then you may, stay until after the meeting and we can chat about the plan.'

Over the next hour we met Pandra O'Malley who told us in no uncertain terms that joining Bulge Busters was really a way for her to meet people, and Magdalena Valentine – recently disabled after she slipped at a pole dancing course – with her niece Alice in tow. If you've ever seen a young slip of a girl help a twenty-plus stone woman onto a weighing scale then you'll know that to watch it is painful. I couldn't believe my eyes as Magdalena heaved herself up, using Alice's arm like a lever until she could balance on the table and weigh herself. The scales beeped and the entire room watched entranced as Jenny said to her, she said, 'You've lost another half a pound this week, Magda, how've you done that?'

Magdalena winked, she's never been one for etiquette has Magdalena, and she said, announcing it to the room as though she were a town crier, she said, 'I've met a nice Italian fella, his name's Raphael, proper arty type – we clicked at a life drawing class, I've got a rather eccentric shape for a woman raised in Partridge Mews.' When she were being wheeled past she spotted me and said, and I was hoping she'd not noticed, she said, "ow do, 'arold, don't see you much down the adult learning centre, now.'

Our Doris piped up at this, she's always been able to defuse any situations that might see me the victim of spousal abuse. And she said to Magdalena, she said, 'It is a shame, Ms Valentine, but our Harold doesn't have much time, what with the garden safari and helping our grandson Theodore with his exams.' Whenever she pronounces the H in my name I feel like she's about to cough something up. She started on it in polite company in the sixties – we'd gone through the whole business at the altar, 'I Doris Thistlethwaite, take thee, 'arold Copeland,' and then we reached the reception and she started calling herself Mrs Harold Copeland and it was at that point I knew I was doomed. I could feel my heart sink. I took one look at my mother, half-cut on whisky, and I said to our Doris, I said to her, 'What are you doing pronouncing the H in my name, our Doris, you've never minded before.'

And her response will stick with me until the day I die because it's the response that sealed my fate. Our Doris said to me, she said, 'I have aspirations, our 'arold, and they most certainly don't stretch to dropping your H in front of company.'

There she sat talking when Magdalena cut off and said to her, she said, 'Must be off, Mrs Copeland, our Alice 'ere has to get back to Partridge Grove, she's working as a social worker.'

I offered a smile – that's another problem with getting older, everyone who was a baby when I became an adult is now an adult themselves and I'm the one who can't chew hard foods – I said to Alice, I said, 'We thought you'd do well, you've always been good with people, should be proud of yourself, Alice.'

'Thanks, Mr Copeland. What're you doing here

anyway, you're as thin as a runner bean?'

'We are here,' our Doris said, 'on an official capacity for the Women's Institute to raise awareness for the garden safari. I will attend a few classes in order to show other members of the community that anything is possible if you have the correct attitude.'

Magdalena snorted, practically fell out of her wheelchair and slammed her hand on the arm of our Doris's chair, she said to her, she said, 'That's your story and you're sticking to it, eh, Doris? Oh I remember when we were at grammar school together – remember you'd get that lad to sneak pork pies in for us from Mrs Joneses? I think that's where my problem must have started, I've always been attracted to danger and there were nothing more dangerous than being caught with pastry in Mrs Atkins' French class.' And with that Alice wheeled Magdalena out of the church hall and our Doris looked more like a beetroot than she ever had done before.

I said to her, I said, 'What's this about pork pies, our Doris?'

And she gave me the Look, her eyes back in her head, fists clenched, cheeks fit to exploding, I could almost see the steam rising from her forehead, she said to me, she said, 'Don't you dare repeat that story to anyone else if you value your miserable life, our 'arold. Making friends with Magdalena Valentine was my biggest regret about my days in education and I do not need to be reminded of every indiscretion I ever made when I was but a child.'

I weren't going to remind her who else I knew who had a hankering for pork pies. Instead, after I'd taken our Doris home to look at the plan in more detail, I beggared off down to the pub. Alf were waiting for me when I got here, I'm getting the hand of this texting lark. I said to him, I said, 'Did you used to steal pork pies for our Doris?'

He chuckled, as he handed me my pint and said to me, he said, 'Now how did you find out about that?'

I slurped my bitter and said, 'Magdalena – what went on there then? If you'd have had it off with our Doris things might have gone differently. I might still have my own teeth!'

'I never really had a thing for your Doris. We lived on the same street and her Dad liked me to keep an eye on her – besides you saw her Mavis, she'd have slaughtered me if I'd so much as gone near. You should think yourself lucky that you were brought up lower middle class.'

'My Uncle Ronald always said as there was no such thing as the middle classes, just lower class folk with too much time on their hands.'

Alf nodded. 'Exactly what someone higher class would say – you had quiche before anyone else on Shakespeare Avenue.'

I said to him, I said, 'There's not much chance of pork pies in our house anymore, anyway. Our Doris had us at Bulge Busters this morning, has it in her head that she can be an inspiration to the women of Partridge Mews.' I shook my head and eyed the menu on the chalk board above the bar, wondering if any of our Doris's spies would tell on me if I were to splash out on steak pie and chips.

As though reading my mind Linda said to me, she said, 'There's no point looking at the food, 'arold, we've had strict warning from your Doris, if you want anything to eat it's salad.'

'Salad and chips?' Alf questioned, a certain quirk to

his eye-brows.

'What if I were starving? That Jenny said as I didn't need to lose any weight.'

Linda shrugged and said to me, she said, 'I'm sorry, 'arold, but I'm more afraid of your Doris than I am of your hunger.' And with that she swept back into the kitchen to collect Mrs Kenilworth's lasagne.

And that's when I slumped down in my chair like a soufflé falling in on itself and I said to Alf, I said, 'I can't wait for this garden safari to be over, I think I've only lost weight because our Doris makes me keep a look out for slugs. It'd be all right if she did any of the bleeding gardening – I mean there's not much doing in daytime television, but sitting in a deck chair reading Jo Nesbo only has me wishing for snow.'

'She's definitely back in the safari then?'

'Something went on between Violet Grey and our Doris after all that business with Janice Dooley - heard anything from her?'

'No one's seen hide nor hair of her since your Doris told the church hall that she were nothing but a smutty liar.' Alf finished the rest of his pint and disappeared – he said as he had some business at the library which could only mean he was going to steal tea and biscuits from the reading group.

I arrived home to discover our Doris sat at the kitchen table, a pile of frozen food in front of her and a cold blast of air coming from the freezer. I said to her, I said, 'What's going on here then, our Doris?'

She sank down into her chair like her spine had been surgically removed and she said to me, she said, 'There's nothing to eat in the freezer, our 'arold.'

I said, 'I can see that, it's all on the blithering table.'

She planted her head in her hands then and I knew

something must be wrong because our Doris won't ruin a perm for anybody – she once went in for an appendectomy and made sure they'd let her wear a shower cap. She groaned and said to me, 'No, 'arold, I've looked in that woman's bloody book – there's nothing I can eat. If I want to lose weight – and I do not need to lose weight, but as I said it's all about motivating the other women in Partridge Mews – then I need less red meat, our freezer's full of steak and burgers and tofu, why do we have tofu, our 'arold?'

'You wanted to impress one of the vegans at the WI and then she went to Alethea Leadbetter's place instead. We kept the tofu in case your Mavis had another one of her phases.'

'She's got a sensitive constitution.'

I rolled my eyes at this and kept my mouth shut. Mavis Thistlewaite runs a café in Wren's Lea, it's a nice little place, but if you order tea you're likely to get poisoned. There's nothing wrong with her constitution; when Edwina Currie were going on about eggs Mavis put a board out saying cheese omelette, now with added salmonella and charged an extra fifty pence. Nobody bothered to point it out because everyone remembers when Mavis threw a temperature gauge through Ernie MacPherson's left eye-brow after he offended her puff pastry.

Instead of reiterating all of this information to our Doris, I said to her, I said, 'What are you going to do with all this frozen food, our Doris? I'm sure you can have it – everything in moderation, isn't that what they always say.'

'It won't look good if I show up next week and say I spent the best part of a week eating coq au vin.'

'It's chicken.'

'That's not the point, our 'arold, as you're very much aware.' Our Doris patted the back of her head to make sure her perm were straight and looked me dead in the eye. She said to me, she said, 'We will donate all of this food to the old folk's home – lord knows they could do with something other than stewed pears – then we'll go to Holland and Barrett, I've always fancied finding out what quinoa is.'

'It's a grain,' I said to her.

She gave me something like a smile and said to me, she said, 'Have you been reading the book, 'arold, how supportive of you, I am pleased that you wish to join me on your weight loss journey even though it was made quite apparent you'd do just as well maintaining.' I could see her eyeing me up and I thought she was going to eat me alive. There was a time when that would have excited me but since I turned seventy I've been hit with this worry; it's a worry that all men must be faced with, it's nothing to do with impotence, it's the worry that if you do start getting amorous you'll have a stroke, she'll think it's an orgasm and leave you to your own devices. No, sexual endeavours are all much more suited to the youngsters, they've more time on their hands for frivolities.

I said to our Doris, I said to her, 'Shall I get the bags out of the car then?'

Our Doris's shoulders visibly slumped but I thought it were probably for the best – she's that fiery she could probably sustain sex until it became tantric but I'm not prepared to risk my life, even if it does involve matting her Silvakrinned perm.

Once the bags were packed we set off down the old folk's home. I thought it a waste of food but I didn't mention anything to our Doris. When Bulge

Busters first came to town in the seventies – our Doris had just had our Angela and wanted to lose some of the maternity weight – she went along, and I were on the diet with her then as well. There's not so much you can do with broccoli but I must have had it every day for two weeks – breakfast, lunch, and dinner – she'd grate it into pasta and scatter it in organic Greek yoghurt and we were having none of it. Eventually, our Doris decided to take up jogging with Cassandra Barlow as she could leave Angela with my Mum on Tuesday mornings. It were for the best, at our Doris's last meeting she were about two inches from launching the leader out of the window.

The food were dropped off at the old folk's home and they couldn't have thanked us more profusely. I said to the young girl at reception, I said to her, 'Now you remember that's home-made coq au vin, it cost me an arm and a leg and all so I could watch Charlie Dimmock, I only want it going to folk who'll respect it for what it is. I don't want it liquidised, or pulped, I've got dentures myself and I managed it just fine.'

Our Doris gave me the Look and said to me, she said, 'Do forgive my husband, he's forgotten himself. Sometimes I believe he would do better in a place like this myself.'

I said to her, I said, 'Who'd drive you around if you put me in a home, our Doris?'

The fact was I felt a bit put out. I could understand our Doris wanting to lose weight – I didn't care for the reasons, I've always gone along with her whims but I spent hard-earned time and money on that coq au vin and she was going to give it to folk so far gone they could have been eating dish water; it were like giving prime steak to a shih tzu.

I said to our Doris on the way out, I said to her, 'I don't want to go to Bulge Busters, our Doris.'

And she said to me, she said, 'This is for the garden safari, our 'arold, you know how much this means to me.'

I couldn't say anything. The last time I mentioned the garden safari she beggared off to Mavis's and left me to pick up the pieces. We'd been working on the garden for that long I were beginning to forget what Charlie Dimmock looked like – the memory of her in that tight green t-shirt were all that got me through most days and I didn't want to think it was all for nothing. If our Doris didn't lose her weight then she'd be a nightmare to live with; I had to be supportive. I was going to the health food shop.

I'd have to get used to quinoa.

Our Doris asked the assistant to find her quinoa. When the lad showed us the stuff – in a giant see through bag looking decidedly bland and in need of a good boiling – he said to us, he said, 'You can buy quinoa ready-made from the supermarket, this is more for your advanced sort of vegan – the ones who won't wear leather.'

I turned to our Doris and said to her, I said, 'You didn't like being a vegan, our Doris, don't you remember Marcia?'

But our Doris weren't listening, she were inside her own world as she heaved three bags of plain quinoa into the basket and went in search of supplements. We ended up with prune juice and seeds that looked more like bird food, unfit for human consumption is what it was, unfit for human consumption and then out of nowhere our Doris flings a ton of liquorice into the basket as though all this food weren't going to keep us regular enough. I said to her, I said, 'Is that what you plan on doing then, our Doris, spending that much time on the toilet you won't be able to eat?'

She gave me the Look and turned back to the assistant, she said to him, she said, 'Do forgive my husband, he isn't accustomed to change – we didn't have colour television until nineteen-eighty-three and even then it was only because the old one kept cutting out during University Challenge.'

I knew I must have been grumpy if our Doris were speaking to common folk. I kept quiet until we got home, paid the lad and left the shop. It might have only been a short drive back from town but it felt as though we were trekking across the Gobi desert. I felt like I were making too many changes for our Doris and she thought she were doing her wifely duties. Maybe it were my own fault for not reading the signals – maybe I should have risked a stroke and gone to bed; our Doris looks a right show stopper in a silk blouse, it clings in all the right places – but this weren't about sex, it were about quinoa and if it's anything like the last faddy food we had in our house, it were going to make mincemeat of my Fixadent.

The next week felt nothing short of torture. I gave up with the quinoa after three days and started sneaking jelly babies into my shed. Our Doris grew angrier by the day. On the fourth day, she barely left the lavatory, except to answer correspondence to the Partridge Mews Gazette and even then she had to stop mid-sentence for a quick one. I said to her, I said, 'I told you this would happen, our Doris – quinoa weren't meant for older folk, we should be on turkey rashers and asparagus.'

She said that if I knew what was good for me I'd

go to the pub.

By the sixth day our Doris were flagging. She'd taken to brisk walking up and down the road – claimed she was trying to see what her at number forty-two were doing with the postman, but we all knew it wasn't. I watched the other residents of Shakespeare Avenue as they gathered on the street to observe a seventy-two year old woman hobble quickly down the pavement. Her perm were definitely lost now – she had flyaway hairs, looking as though a ball of wool were unravelling on top of her head. I didn't notice until her twelfth circuit around the house that she wore odd trainers. There were more sweat on her body now than there had been on our wedding night, albeit this time I wasn't drunk and trying to hang my socks from a balcony in Blackpool.

I said to her, I said, 'You'll be doing yourself a mischief in odd shoes, our Doris.'

She tried something similar to the Look but gave up on the third go and said to me, as she passed, she said, 'I saw it on Lorraine Kelly and you know how I won't watch that woman unless she has something profitable to say. Odd shoes means your body has to work that bit harder to work off calories.'

'People are watching you out there.'

'Good,' she said, she said to me, 'if they're watching then I'm inspiring them enough to think. I am going to work hard for my body, our 'arold and don't you forget it.'

I said to her, I said, 'You're seventy-two.'

'I still have a body, don't I? Just because I'm seventy-two doesn't mean I can't be a sex symbol, I'm a fetish now, 'arold, if I wanted to sell my body I could make millions.'

'The only way we're making money from our bodies is through medical science,' I said to her.

And she said to me, she said, 'Yes, we've no reason to resort to Janice Dooley measures now do we?'

She'd cursed herself. I don't know how she'd done it. Someone must have overhead us talking – the front door were open and folk from all over were watching her as she tried to eke out those last few pounds. As we walked into the Bulge Busters meeting the next day who should be there but the great pariah of Little Street, Janice Dooley herself. She were wearing a low-cut blouse showing too much of her sunburnt chest and a skirt that was little more than a lampshade.

Our Doris set her shoulders back and said to her, she said, 'I am exceptionally pleased to see you, Miss Dooley, I do hope we can set aside our differences as we march forward with our plans for the garden safari.'

They were in the line at this point, I'd made the coffee and were sat at a table close by. I watched Janice lean in close and prepared to jump into action – not that I could do much, by the time I got to my feet one of them could have been face first in a cardboard cutout. And Janice squared up to our Doris and she said to her, she said, 'I wouldn't know much about the garden safari, Doris. After the big reveal I was given my marching orders, as well you know – so why don't you keep your poncey nose out of my business and I will sure as Hell make sure that I steer clear of yours.'

When Janice stepped up to weigh I saw our Doris lean in slightly, her eyes wide and a smile crept up her face until Jenny piped up with, she said to Janice, 'That's brilliant, Jan, you've done fantastic – five pounds in one week – we could all learn a lot from you.'

Janice glared at our Doris with a look that could have made Little Street freeze over and she said, to no one in particular, she said, 'I've always been naturally toned – it's one of the perks of not constantly having my nose up somebody else's backside.'

And our Doris said, and I knew she wanted her to hear as she stepped onto the scales, 'I do suppose you have endured a lot of extra-curricular activities, Miss Dooley, all that extra training with Mr Gadsden.'

The smirk were soon wiped from our Doris's face when Jenny piped up with, she said, 'I'm sorry, Mrs Copeland, but you've gained two pounds.'

Our Doris's face fell – her eyebrows folded together as though a caterpillar crawled across her forehead. She hopped off the scales and back again – the beep and the same response from Jenny.

When Janice Dooley spoke I knew we were all done for. I knew it were the end – I thought were all going to end up six feet under, our Doris would bury us in the graveyard herself. Janice Dooley said to her, she said, 'Cheer up, Doris, if you'd been up to more extracurricular activities maybe you'd have lost some weight – I suppose it's the big head that does it.'

And that's when the scales flew across the room.

Jenny screamed.

I yelled our Doris's name but it was no use.

The scales flew through the air and we watched as Janice Dooley of Little Street was hit in the chest and catapulted into a trestle table full of low-fat cereal bars.

Before I knew what was happening, our Doris were on top of her and her fists were doing things they've never done before, and clumps of hair were on the floor and our Doris and Janice were rolling across the lino screaming at one another and Janice had her shoes in her hands and was beating our Doris across the back, who had completely forgotten she was wearing her Laura Ashley blazer with matching plimsolls because she was using them to beat Janice Dooley across her extremely bruised chest.

Back in the sixties when Janice Dooley and our Doris first started stepping out in town everyone anticipated a brawl at some point. We started making bets. I lost ten quid to Bobby Flynn because they didn't attack each other at the wedding reception.

Fifty years down the line, both of them in their seventies, no one could have expected it. Partridge Mews finally had what it had always been hoping for – and there was no stopping the two women now, even when our Doris rocketed Janice through the fire escape into the churchyard.

Folk stopped on the street outside to watch through the bars as the two of them hid behind graves and flung stones and shoes and mud at each other before running and dragging each other into the dirt.

When the police arrived I knew we were all done for.

9

TRiAL

Our Doris has been charged with GBH and public indecency. After she was arrested for attacking Janice Dooley of Little Street, she forwent her lawyer's advice to keep her mouth shut and told the police, she said to them, she said, 'If you'd have been a few minutes later, I'd have made sure she'd never set foot in Partridge Mews again, let alone Little Street.' Luckily, Ira Murgatroyd, the lawyer, told them that she was still hyped up after all the adrenaline and distress caused by Janice and our Doris isn't facing a charge of attempted murder.

She wasn't happy when she found out they were releasing her and keeping Janice Dooley in police custody as this was her third arrest in as many weeks. Apparently Janice has been going after members of the Partridge Mews Women's Institute; Rene Thomason barely got away with her eye-brows after Janice snuck into the beauticians and applied depilatory cream instead of hot wax.

Our Doris had spent long enough in a cell anyway, her clothes were taken as evidence and she were brought to me in a grey tracksuit. I said to her, I said, 'Let's get you home,' and she didn't reply as I lead her towards the car.

Once we got home, I went straight through to the kitchen and heard our Doris pottering about upstairs, her footsteps hushed as she slipped into the bathroom and locked the door. When I heard the bath start up with a rush of water that could have blown up the immersion, I knew our Doris was planning something.

I did what all red-blooded Northerners do in those situations, I went into the kitchen and put the kettle on. When our Doris has guests around she brings out the teapot but desperate times called for desperate measures and I took the two matching blue mugs out of the top cupboard and planted teabags in each of them – I added sugar to mine and went into a debate about our Doris. Did spending a night in a police cell count as shock? I didn't find an answer but three heaped spoonfuls of the sweet stuff found its way into our Doris's mug.

Then, like the number twelve bus, all my dilemmas arrived at once.

I opened the fridge and made the unwelcome discovery that we were out of milk. As a newcomer to Bulge Busters, our Doris decided that milk, no matter the variety, full-fat, semi-skimmed, skimmed, soya, almond, coconut, hazelnut, it could come from the left nipple of a fat-free platypus and our Doris, ever-diligent where her weight was concerned, wouldn't have it near her fridge; not that week in any case.

Our Doris would spend the best part of an hour in

the bath; she's mastered the art over the last fifty years, I once said to her, I said, 'No wonder you've got so many wrinkles, the amount of time you spent underwater.'

She glanced at me from under her towel-turban, and it were but a glance, when she said to me, she said, 'No wonder you've got haemorrhoids the amount of time you spend on the toilet.'

When you've been married for a few months you come to the realisation that the only alone time you'll ever get is when you're in the bathroom. I'd mastered the art of finishing crosswords, tax returns, Tom Clancy's, making holiday plans, and polishing, all from the comfort of our Twifords toilet.

Being able to hide sounded preferable to going out into Partridge Mews. Getting my coat from the hook by the front door I could envisage Indigo down the corner shop – daughter of Sandra Marsden, who went through a well-documented rebellious stage in her twenties that resulted in the closure of the Partridge Mews YMCA – she'd ask after our Doris, all fluttering false eye-lashes and swathes of sheer fabric that look as though she's just robbed a haberdashery, and she'd say to me, gleaning information to tell her grandmother down the home, she'd say to me, 'How's the missis, Mr Copeland?' And I'd have to think carefully about my answer because anything I said would ultimately come back on our Doris and then word would reach our Doris and she would corner me in the kitchen.

But that couldn't be helped, not with the current milk situation.

Neither could the five people who stood on the step as I opened the front door. Assembled before me like knights of the round table stood our Angela, Theo,

Alf and his Edith, and Violet Grey, all with an assortment of food, from fresh baked pastries from Dennings, Tesco pork pies, and a picnic basket with a baguette spear to what I saw underneath Alf's arm. He saw me look and raised it with a twinkle in his eye. 'You've been out all night and I weren't scuppering my chances of a brew.'

I said to them, and there were a mild lift in my heart that wasn't angina, I said, 'What're you all here for?'

Violet Grey handed me the picnic basket, all regal aplomb, and she said to me, she said, 'Doris has been my dear friend for over half a century, she helped me when Miss Dooley tried to besmirch my husband's character and I will help her in this. I brought all the ingredients for a correct bruschetta, and, forgive me for being stoically British, a picnic – there should be enough sandwiches to make do.'

I didn't know what to say, there were no words left in my throat, I were choked up, I'd never had to cope with Violet Grey on my own before.

And out of nowhere, our Theo took the picnic basket from me and turned to Violet, all smiles, his braces doing this funny thing in the sun and he said to her, he said, 'I'm sure my grandfather would issue you with the correct compliments as befitting a man his social standing, but you can understand that he has been through a great shock. Please follow us through to the kitchen where we can peruse your most delectable dishes.'

'I should hope we will do much more than peruse them but I appreciate the sentiment all the same.' She followed our Theo, Angela and Edith into the kitchen leaving me stood there with Alf.

He winked at me and said, he said, 'That grandson of yours should go into politics – with a tongue like that he'll give your Doris a run for her money.'

I wasn't sure how they would help our Doris, but one thing was for sure, I'd need to find that teapot.

Once we'd settled into the kitchen, tea cups full – me halfway through a pork pie – our Doris came into the room. She'd clearly heard all the commotion, dressed in a floral print dress and pastel blue blazer, with a scarf around her throat but not tied – it's an outfit she still doesn't think she's mastered, the 'wasn't expecting visitors' look because our Doris is always ready for any possible Partridge Mews resident to knock at the door – she considered installing CCTV once just to make sure no undesirables walked along her garden path.

Now she stood there, face the picture of a woman acknowledging her mistakes, all meek smiles and a bit of a twinkle in her eyes that erred caution and didn't veer into triumphant, and she said to us, she said, 'It fills my heart to know that our friends and family would gather at such a traumatic time. It will be no secret in the town that I have committed a crime – I did – yesterday morning I attacked Janice Dooley of Little Street at a Bulge Busters meeting taking place at the church hall. I do not regret my actions. I fully intended to harm Miss Dooley and if the opportunity arose would happily do so again for she is nothing if not a stain on this society. However, I know that the best attacks I can make are that of the verbal variety and therefore, I ask that you help me in this difficult time.'

Violet Grey rose to her feet, wiping her fingers clean on a handkerchief she unleashed from under her sleeve. She set her hand on our Doris's shoulder and said to her, she said, 'Now listen here, Mrs Copeland, you and I have been through much in this fair town of ours, I never for one moment believed that Erin Beaumont would name her child Red but she did, yet we managed to get his name changed, through several letters to the Partridge Mews Gazette and a campaign that saw Granada Reports on the Beaumont's doorstep.

'Janice Dooley of Little Street, we all agree, is a menace that must be stopped. We have the people of Partridge Mews behind us. We managed to eradicate Bartholomew Wicks' ridiculous hairstyle, you will receive a minimal sentence, Mrs Copeland, I promise you that.'

Silence fell in the kitchen. Never before had we seen Violet Grey as forthright. I thought she must have ruined seventy plus years' worth of keeping her nose in the air and her lips pursed. I'm sure I saw wrinkles burst on her face, deep tracks treading through her face as though her Oil of Olay had stopped working.

Our Doris offered Violet something like a smile and said to her, she said, 'What about the garden safari?'

'What of it?' Violet said, 'You made an impassioned speech at Janice Dooley's abdication and I will value that now as I uphold the offer you received of the fifth house in our final garden safari.'

If our Doris had ever had eyes wider it were in the five minutes I left the room whilst she were in labour. Her eyes practically left their sockets – you could have used them for golf they were that prominent – and she said to her, she said, 'What do you mean, final garden safari?'

Violet smiled meekly and I realised that this served them both somehow; Violet had something planned and she weren't telling us about it. That must have been why she were being so kind; she'd tried it once in nineteen-seventy-two when me and our Doris were talking about getting a conservatory. She started being kind, brought around the odd quiche and over time intimated that weren't conservatories a bit lower-middle-class?

Our Doris, ever one to want to be decidedly upper class decided we didn't need a conservatory as it would ruin the charm of our otherwise splendid Victorian home. Two weeks later the Greys put in plans for a conservatory and we saw neither hide nor hair of Violet Grey until she invited us around to celebrate the erection of her conservatory; an event we had to attend as it was the height of the social calendar that year.

Now, in the kitchen, we were all on tenterhooks. Alf's pork pie dripped piccalilli onto the counter and Edith didn't hastily swipe it away with a convenient dishcloth – Theo had stopped live tweeting the conversation, his phone that close to his coffee it was almost a spoon. Angela's eyes darted from our Doris to Violet and back again, her mouth opening and closing as though she were eating a phantom doughnut.

And Violet Grey was proud here. She'd got her head tilted just so and her shoulders were back, her hands closed across her stomach – the picture of Princess Anne – and she said to our Doris, a declaration to us all, she said, 'The committee has spoken and decided that this year will serve as the last garden safari due to the surrounding controversy.'

I turned away from the crushed pork pie in Alf's hand and looked at our Doris.

I should have kept my eyes where they were.

I could have stopped him.

Instead I sat and watched as several pork pies and

tablespoons of piccalilli hit Violet Grey in the back of the head. She spun around to see our Angela, Theo, Edith and Alf stood there, all bearing arms, and Alf's eyes were wild – he looked like Worzel Gummidge having a seizure – and he said to her, he practically yelled, he said, 'We all know what's going on here – the garden safari hasn't been the big success you'd hoped. Not enough people care about traipsing around the posh end of Partridge Mews in the hopes of seeing how far up your bosovers your bleeding heads are. If they want to see things that acrobatic they'd turn on Britain's Got Talent. Well I can tell you something now Mrs Grey, you are not blaming our Doris for your mess – your garden safari failed because of your poor management.'

Violet Grey, trying to maintain her decorum as a blob of piccalilli slipped down her shoulders, said to Alf, she said, 'I'll have you know that I have managed many successful events in Partridge Mews.'

'I'm afraid that's not quite true, is it, Mrs Grey?' Edith ran her hands under her tap as she spoke, all hints of her crime washed away. She said to Violet, she said, 'You use other people to your own gains – you are all about the delegating rather than the actual work. Mrs Copeland here has arranged more galas, tea dances and sport's days than you've arranged excuses for your husband's whereabouts.' She smiled here and I realised that I didn't give Edith the credit she was due. She continued, she said, 'But we're not here to discuss your husband's infidelities – we're here to help Mrs Copeland with the planning for her upcoming court case. If we hear of any excuses of controversy, we will see to it that the people of Partridge Mews believe the controversy stems from the breakdown of your marriage.'

'Mrs Simpson, I assure you my marriage is not breaking down.'

'I do not disagree with you, Mrs Grey, however we have steered clear of discussing Mr Grey's whereabouts in the streets, we have yet to mention the slight hints of sherry on your breath – Janice Dooley planted a seed we have not acknowledged, but blame Mrs Copeland, Violet, and I will ensure it takes root.'

Violet didn't let the silence linger. She looked our Doris straight in the eye and said to her, she said, 'I will leave the few food stuffs I brought as a gift to you. I'll telephone to intimate collection details for the basket.' After a fleeting glance around the room she added, she said, 'Enjoy it while you can.'

She left.

Our Doris and I exchanged a look that only a husband and wife can share.

Over the next few hours we made plans. Theo thought that he could get our Doris's side of the story on film and post it to YouTube. Our Angela thought the best bet would be for our Doris to appear all over the place doing nice deeds – having conversations with folk she doesn't usually talk to. Alf considered pulling off an even bigger crime to draw more attention to himself but Edith thought that'd ruin their grandson's chances of a promotion.

Once they'd left I locked the door, faced our Doris and said to them, I said, 'If that's the best we've got our Doris, you're beggared.'

Our Doris gave me the Look and said to me, she said, 'I bleeding well know that, our 'arold but someone had to put Violet Grey in her place and it sure as Hell wasn't going to be you, was it? There's nothing I can say now that'll get her back on side. It's a good job this is my forte – our first plan of action is to get me on the front page of the Partridge Mews Gazette, I'll telephone them now.'

Now I hate being the bearer of bad news but I said to her, I said, 'You attacked a reporter, our Doris, they'll revel in this, they will.'

Our Doris's shoulders slumped and she leant in the door frame of the kitchen, and I wasn't prepared – I hadn't seen our Doris cry since her great aunt Ida's funeral – and there she stood in the doorway, her back trembling as she cried, using her scarf as a mop and she said to me, she said, 'I'm not made for this, our 'arold, I'm Doris Copeland – I'm supposed to be a pillar of the community and I'm a laughing stock.'

I had my arms around her shoulders and lead her into the sitting room. I said to her, and I think it was our marital vows that saved me, I said, 'You did wrong, our Doris, there's no getting past that. We don't need the Gazette, we have the WI, we have the boys down the allotment – we have Partridge Mews – Janice Dooley has Little Street and since when has that done anyone any good?'

Our Doris sniffed once more and she said to me, and there were a glint of something in her eye, she said, 'That might be the smartest thing you ever said, 'arold Copeland.'

We sat there a few more minutes, her leaning against my shoulder in a fashion we hadn't tried since our courting days down the flicks, and I said to her, I said, 'We best get to work then.'

The next morning I woke up to find our Doris on the phone. She doesn't usually let me sleep in, claims that it leads to an unwarranted takeover of the duvet and she didn't spend fifty years of marriage not to create a fair distribution of the bed sheets. I kept my eyes shut and listened to our Doris downstairs as she put the phone back in its cradle and climbed the stairs.

She opened the bedroom door and said to me, she said, 'Get yourself up, our 'arold, I know you're awake – you're not breathing like a hippopotamus is sat on your chest. Anyway, Ira Murgatroyd just rang, my trial is next week, the judge had an opening apparently.'

It were the nonchalance that got me; I flung myself out of bed and said to her, I said, 'Next week? How are we meant to get the Gazette on side by then?'

Since our Doris's outburst with the secateurs the editor of the Partridge Mews Gazette had taken to responding to each and every missive our Doris sent his way. When she questioned Tiffany Bethnal's use of braised Philadelphia as an hors d'oeuvre he commented, he wrote for all the world to see, Editor's Note: although Mrs Copeland may raise a valid point about high calorie foodstuffs at children's school discos, she, herself, served a prawn cocktail starter in the early two-thousands – a move that was seen by some as nostalgic and by others as woefully behind the times – quoted verbatim from Mrs Pandra O'Malley's article in 2002's June twenty-fifth edition.

Of course our Doris continued to send her letters. I said to her, I said, 'Why don't you write to the Courier instead?'

That got me the Look, and she said to me, she said, 'I wouldn't use the Courier to puppy train an Alsatian – it's a rag – no substance, no merit, and you'd do well to remember that, our 'arold.'

And she stuck with the Gazette.

I didn't think too much about any form of

grovelling. But our Doris said to me, and I suppose it were obvious really, she said, 'They won't outwardly discredit me, our 'arold, I'm their most consistent contributor since little Billy Earl, they'd be mad to turn their back on me.'

When we went downstairs we weren't prepared for the newspaper on the mat. Our Doris was on the front page of the Partridge Mews Gazette laying into Janice Dooley. The headline weren't pretty, 'Mrs Copeland's Graveyard Brawl.'

I thought our Doris would issue a retort; I looked for the defiant set of her shoulders, the gleam in her eye, her clenched fists ... but there were none of that.

Our Doris clapped her hands to her sides and said, she said, 'Well that's that then.'

I retrieved the newspaper and followed her into the kitchen, reading as I went, the paper were claiming that the day's issue revealed the innermost secrets of the town's most distinguished citizens. I said to our Doris, I said, 'You must have really upset them, our Doris.'

'Of course I bleeding upset them, our 'arold, I attacked one of their reporters with a dictionary and a pair of secateurs, what's surprising is that they haven't got Janice Dooley of bleeding Little Street as a page three girl offering an exclusive on her side of the story.'

After a quick flick to the third page, I made a brew. I said our Doris, I said, 'There's still the lads down the allotment – and you have –'

I stopped there. I could not believe my eyes. In fifty years of marriage to our Doris I never expected to witness what I saw emblazoned on pages five and six.

Our Doris had the look she gets when I'm shifty, the old quirked eye-brow and she said to me, she said, 'What is it, our 'arold.'

My lips were positively trembling as I said it –
because the cat were out of the bag, the big secret had
been revealed. 'Violet's revealed Doug's affair.'

Our Doris were furious. The Grey's had surpassed
us again.

It took our Doris most of the day to calm down.

After lunch she muttered something inaudible but
altogether she were that angry she were rendered mute.
Then, when I were just settling down to watch Tipping
Point she said to me, she said, 'I don't know whether
it's an act of friendship or Violet refusing to let us have
a hold over her.'

I must have looked startled as I said to her, I said,
'How can it be an act of friendship, our Doris?'

'Because if she cancels due to controversy folk will
assume it's due to her marital breakdown. But it could
be a way of her having all control. You forget, 'arold,
it's all how folk see something. They're not seeing a
woman wronged, they're seeing a woman who couldn't
get her husband to stay faithful.'

I said to her, I said, 'But it's not her fault.'

She shrugged at me and said, 'It'll be seen as the
ultimate failure. I don't know why she did it.'

I didn't have to wait long to find out. I'd bobbed
down to the Hare and Horse to have a few drinks with
Alf when Violet Grey appeared sentry-like, looking
every inch the Anna Karenina. She stood over our table
and she said to Alf, she said, 'Alfred, I wonder whether
you might go and purchase me a beverage, I am quite
accustomed to a gin and tonic. Take your time.'

And she handed him a twenty pound note.

A twenty pound note.

No one hands twenty pound notes to Alf because
lord knows they'll never see the change. And as he ran

to the bar, she sat down in his seat and met my eyes.

I said to her, I said, 'You shouldn't have done that.'

Violet Grey shrugged and set her hands on the table. She still wore her wedding ring. She said to me, she said, 'I need to discuss some things with you, Mr Copeland.'

'I'm not sure our Doris would be too happy to hear we'd been chatting.'

And she said to me, she said, 'This concerns Mrs Copeland – you will have seen the big reveal in the newspaper no doubt?'

I slurped my bitter and nodded. 'Bit of a bold move, wasn't it?' I said to her.

Her gaze dropped then and she said, 'I have good reason. You see, Mr Copeland, I am leaving Partridge Mews.'

The pub were silent. Violet had chosen me because she and our Doris were pillars of the community and today both of them had fallen into disrepute. Everyone would be listening to hear any iota of gossip and I, Harold Copeland, resident of Partridge Mews who can never seem to get a day's peace would have to be a means to an end.

I thought to myself, 'what would our Doris do?' and straightened my spine, though I were sure that uncoiling my vertebrae might set my arthritis on edge. I straightened my cardigan and I said to Violet, I said, 'I suppose that Doug won't be coming with you?'

She shook her head. 'You're a man, Mr Copeland, you'll never understand. However, my departure means that the Partridge Mews Women's Institute will require a new chairwoman and I would like for your wife, Mrs Copeland, to be my successor.'

I must have been gobsmacked – the hush of

whispers filled the pub – Alf stood at the bar, waiting for the gin and tonic and I sat staring at Violet. I said to her, and I were completely dumbfounded, I said, 'But the court case.'

'I know the judge. Mrs Copeland cannot be given too serious a sentence and the WI will see that she was provoked by one who you will note is still in a cell. I needed enough controversy to draw attention away from her, I hope that you can understand.' She stood up and crossed the pub, took her drink from Alf and brought it to her lips before handing it back and saying to him, she said, 'Do you know, I have had the sudden revelation that alcohol can be ruinous, please enjoy this drink on behalf of myself and my former partner Douglas.'

And with a final fleeting glance at the Hare and Horse, Violet Grey left the pub and Partridge Mews.

'She'll have gone to visit her sister,' our Doris said to me when I got home. I'd given her all the information as soon as I'd arrived, making sure she'd taken a seat in the lounge, and kept anything breakable away from her throwing arm.

I had sweet tea in my hand and said to her, I said, 'You don't seem surprised, our Doris.'

'When have you known Violet Grey to court controversy? Even when she caught her stilettos in her gypsy skirt in the Easter tea dance of nineteen-seventy-three she intimated that she had always meant to make the faux pas so as people could see that she was a normal human being.'

'She's spoken to your judge, our Doris.'

'I thought she might.'

'Do you want to talk about it?'

She sat for a moment before saying to me, she said,

'I've decided that we do not need the support of Partridge Mews to help lessen my sentence. I committed a crime and will pay the consequences.'

Which is exactly what she told the judge the following week. She'd dressed in her best prim old lady – beige two-piece suit and flat black plimsolls with a hint of gold to the buckle. After paying a visit to the salon, she now had a rejuvenated perm and wore delicate make-up so as to give off the air of one who still wants to look their best even in adversity, in this case adversity in the form of Janice Dooley of Little Street who gave a raving tale of how our Doris behaved like a crazed madwoman and it were only through sheer wit that she managed to escape. She hadn't counted on our Doris.

She never does.

It is a mistake Janice has always made that she never anticipates our Doris's attack.

The judge said to her, she said, 'Mrs Copeland, you have pled guilty, do you have anything to say?'

She nodded and said to him, she said, 'Thank you for giving me the opportunity, your honour, though you had no need to do so I appreciate it all the same. I must offer my utmost apologies to Miss Dooley and to the citizens of Partridge Mews for my less-than-exceptional behaviour.

'I let Miss Dooley antagonise me when I should have taken the moral high ground and left the church hall. I deeply regret my actions and thank the Partridge Mews Women's Institute for not losing faith in me and offering me the role of chairwoman. It is not a reward for my wrongdoing but a reminder that I am better than this trial would have many believe, and mean much to many of the women in this town.

'I let the unimportant words of an unimportant person affect me and for that I am incredibly sorry. Thank you.'

Janice Dooley's plum face set off her neck brace brilliantly. Her arms were folded and she must have worked on her scowl because she had the face of a bulldog.

The judge coughed through the chatter in the gallery and she said to our Doris, she said, 'Mrs Copeland, you committed a serious crime against Miss Dooley and though I believe you truly regret your actions and that you have the support of Partridge Mews at this difficult time, I still must award you some penalty. Therefore, I sentence you to one-hundred hours of community service, the terms of which will be decided at a later date. For now, I wish you all the best in your endeavours.'

Our Doris's smile couldn't have been bigger – her teeth practically shone as she sidled across the room and said to me, she said, 'One trial over, one more to go.'

I said to her, 'What do you mean, our Doris?'

She said to me, she said, 'The garden safari of course, a gift to Partridge Mews for their support in this trying time.'

I'm not sure our Doris recognised she'd been sentenced, her head were in the clouds. In two weeks she'd managed to rid herself of two enemies, attacked Janice Dooley of Little Street and succeeded as chairwoman of the WI; there was no way she was going to let something as trivial as community service bring her down.

10

THE FiFTH HOUSE

Our Doris is in a wheelchair for the duration.

After the court case she flung herself into arranging the house for the garden safari, as in, she told me what she wanted and I started spending a lot more time down the allotment. I did think about asking British Gas whether they could re-route some electric so that I could watch television but there's not much doing on daytime television unless you fancy constant repeats of Heartbeat. Either way I have to keep a close eye on Tabitha Melrose's petunias – she's emigrated to the Yemen but doesn't want to give up her patch because it's a beggar to get on the list with the council and she's not sure her new relationship with Sven will work out anyway, says as he has mother issues and she's gone there for the sex not the familial bonds.

Alf were that worried he started bringing me lunch down to the shed. I said to him, I said, 'Do you know I think I should join the WI I've heard that much of its inner workings.'

He handed me a thermos mug of tea and said to me, he said, 'Edith's been spending that much time around your house I keep checking that her toothbrush is still in the pot.'

'I'd noticed.' I'd barely been up five minutes before our Doris were hammering on the bathroom. She yelled at me, she said, 'Hurry up, our 'arold, Edith'll be here in a minute and I don't want the first thing she smells to be your flatulence – I chose this life, I refuse to share it with those who wish to frequent our parlour.'

I shouted back, I said, 'We couldn't afford a parlour, our Doris.'

'If you'd had better aspirations we could have afforded a parlour.'

'I had better aspirations but you held the purse strings – we could have afforded a parlour but who fancied the new mop?'

I couldn't see it but if the Look could burn through bathroom doors I'm sure it was then. As I gargled my mouth wash she said to me, she hissed, 'The Speedclean three-thousand-and-six is specially imported from Switzerland to make it easier for housewives the world over. I refuse to hear a word said against it.'

'For how much that cost, I'm surprised it doesn't come with a ready-printed injunction.'

I ended up at the coffee bar. The barista must have noticed the bags under my eyes because she offered me a free extra shot and brought my panini to the table; I'd ordered bacon and brie because mozzarella, chicken and rocket did not seem like the perfect accompaniment to the eight o'clock news.

She said to me, she said, 'Aren't you that Granny's husband?'

'Which Granny?'

And this is where she got excited, all raised eyebrows and breathy tones as her pace sped up and she said to me, she said, 'The one who attacked Mrs Dooley – me and the girls from the slimming club thought it were great. She were always coming in talking about how she could lose weight quickly – one week she'd be a stone heavier than the next week and she'd try and tell us it were because she hadn't been getting enough vigorous exercise – and now we all know why, don't we? Either way, me and Elspeth think it were bricks.'

I had to admit she had me befuddled. I said to her, I said, 'Bricks?'

She nodded at this and said, 'In her pockets. Anyhow, I don't blame your missus for throwing the scales at her – I've wanted to do it myself a few times – but it did throw them out of sync, they tried to tell me that I were thirty-seven stone, I mean do I look thirty-seven stone, I doubt they'd let me in Sainsbury's if I did.' And she walked away with a, 'Eat your panini before it gets cold,' and a wink.

I've never known something as difficult to chew with dentures as a panini. I bit into it and thought my dentures were stuck, that Fixadent hadn't planned for bread that thin and hard it could fling your teeth across the room faster than any slingshot. I imagine it's what they must call crisp on the continent, then again everything Italian is al dente and that may as well be another word for uncooked.

I considered calling the barista back but didn't want to contend with any more musings on the extra-marital endeavours of Janice Dooley of Little Street. She'd been all over the Gazette talking about how our Doris had always had it in for her – in retaliation our

Doris had sent in previously unseen photographs of Janice from the nineteen-seventies when she'd got absolutely beggared over three bottles of Babycham and a few glasses of Mrs Pickering's home-made elderflower wine. The photographs showed her in various drunken positions and states of undress, she managed to keep her eyes open for two of them – one of them was taken over the top of a stall in the ladies at the church hall which had me thinking our Doris would stop at nothing to get blackmail material.

Since it's now publically known that they can't stand each other they haven't held back in their proclamations of hatred. When it all started, our Doris might have sent a short note to the Gazette talking about how Janice Dooley's dress might have been cut wrong for a children's birthday tea – the week before last she sent one note stating, it said, 'Janice Dooley is nothing short of a harlot in dresses that do nothing for her varicose veins.' That was it – no mention of how she could solve the problem, no intimation that she could improve, just a statement of fact alongside screenshots of security footage showing the scales hitting her in the mid-riff, her collapsed on the trestle table, and another as she struggled to get low-fat porridge oats out of her hair.

A few of the Bulge Busters ladies should have tried the coffee bar, it'd take them that long to chew through the panini, and the hard bacon, and brie like Playdoh – that claggy it stuck my tongue to my gums until I could swill my Americano around my mouth – they'd lose that much weight because their mouths would be out of use for a week. I'm pretty sure I came out of that coffee bar with more blisters than I would have if I'd planted my mouth in a coal fire.

I ended up wandering around town, not doing much. The florist, Mrs Singh, stood outside watering her hanging baskets. When she caught sight of me she beckoned me over with a twitch of her fingers and a yell, she said to me, 'Mr Copeland, get yourself over here this instant!' I don't know what it is about the mothers of Partridge Mews that breeds harridans but we must have more deaf men than the rest of the North West and I'm pretty confident it's all to do with the ululating of wives.

I managed my best smile in any case, wandered across, and I said to Mrs Singh, I said, 'How do, Mrs Singh?'

Well if that didn't summon the most horrendous of faces I don't know what it did. Mrs Singh's face came over all gargoyle and she said to me, she said, 'Do you know what I am wearing?'

I took a moment to look. I'm not that good with noticing the details – I didn't notice about Dame Edna Everage until I started to develop something of a crush and Alf took it upon himself to break the news. Mrs Singh wore a long creamy-looking salwar kameez, with salwar that thin they must have broken a dozen health and safety laws and I said to her, I said, 'It's a salwar kameez, Mrs Singh, I should know you spent three months educating me about it in nineteen-eighty-nine.'

She nodded at this and said to me, she said, 'Exactly, and since then we've gone on to become great friends.'

'I only came in for tomato seeds.'

'It were the look you gave.'

'That weren't at your clothing it were the price, if I'd been buying beanstalk seeds I might have agreed.'

'Anyway,' she said to me with a breath before

continuing, she said, 'that young lad of Ingrid Myrkkleson's went past not fifteen minutes ago spouting forth about how I disgust him and I should be out of my pyjamas by now. I mean how disrespectful – is he entirely ignorant – I should think it's more disgusting to wander about town with his trousers hung that low I can almost see his buttocks chewing his underwear.'

I did something I wouldn't have done in usual circumstances because I like to think that I can be quite kind to folk but I said to Mrs Singh, I said, 'I don't have time for this today, Jacinta, either beat him about the head with a mop bucket or ring his mother but I've got problems of my own.'

And that's when I went to the allotment.

And stayed there.

I couldn't be doing with people. If they're not asking me if I think I can grow a three-hundred year old oak tree in two weeks to block out the unsightly mess that is my shed then they're asking me about our Doris. Ernest Outhwaite actually went so far as to ask whether I could put in a good word for him and have him moved up to fourth house from seventh. I mentioned it to our Doris and she didn't even say anything, just gave me the Look and huffed as though the suggestion weren't worth her time.

I stayed a few hours after Alf left and set off home. When I got there our Doris were in the lounge watching my recorded episodes of Groundforce. I said to her, I said, 'What's for dinner, our Doris?'

And she said to me, and it were a bolt out of the blue it was, she said, 'I've ordered Chinese – it'll be here in about twenty minutes, now get yourself in the kitchen and make a brew, I've been at this for seven hours and I've yet to discover how to grow a clematis.'

I put the kettle on and looked out into the garden that had become something of my pride and joy in the last half a century. When we first moved in it had been nothing more than paving slabs and a few weeds. Me and a few of the lads made it something of a project – I were the first of the lot to be married and once Alf set his sights on Edith's Victoria Sponge he were more than ready to make her Mrs Simpson. We dug out the garden and planted grass seeds, built the shed in the corner where it wouldn't detract from the view of the back kitchen, and our Doris's old man gave me his copy of The Reader's Digest's The Gardening Year.

Over time the garden had become my contribution towards the house, seeing as our Doris wouldn't set foot on the grass as she worried the chlorophyll might ruin her plimsolls and she didn't want me using a hoover as I didn't know how to handle it in a manner befitting the husband of an upper middle-class heterosexual white woman with a penchant for show tunes and PD James.

When she first brought up the garden safari I knew that I would end up doing the majority of the hard grafting. Our Doris got rid of the slugs, but she made sure that no amount of dirt ever touched her dungarees – I think she must have threatened it, made some sort of deal with the devil, that if he made sure her clothes stayed clean he could have the soul of Janice Dooley of Little Street; at least I'd hope she'd choose Janice.

Once the kettle boiled, I made the tea and went back into the lounge. Our Doris had switched over to Channel Three and were watching The Chase. That's when I noticed her clothes – she wore blue jeans – I said to her, I said, 'What's with the denim, our Doris?'

She shrugged and said to me, she said, 'I have a deep clean planned, our 'arold. The certain well-wishers who attend the garden safari will wish to come indoors and I plan on offering them a delightfully delectable feast of multi-cultural cuisine and Quiche Lorraine for the vegans.'

I said to her, I said, 'There's bacon in that, our Doris.'

'Of course there's bacon, they eat nothing but runner beans for three-hundred-and-sixty-five days of the year when they enter the fifth house, our home, after a long day of seeing sub-par gardens, I want them to know that they needn't worry about any societal obligations. Being vegan is all down to peer pressure, our 'arold, and I'll have none of it in my house.'

I were saved by the doorbell and went to collect the Chinese. Our Doris had ordered me something reminiscent of fish, chips and mushy peas; after the panini that morning and Alf's sandwiches which were more like bricks, it was welcome. I said to our Doris, I said, 'Thanks for this, our Doris.'

'Don't be getting any ideas about this, our 'arold, I'll be expecting you in that kitchen tomorrow evening – I'd quite like a salad, nothing too fancy, but a dressing would be nice, and new potatoes, and perhaps some chicken breasts in a mint vinaigrette.'

I chewed my fish and nodded, hoping my eyes hadn't betrayed me. Our Doris always has high expectations of my culinary skills. She shouldn't have worried about the cooking, should have stuck to thinking about whether Modesty Dukesbridge really deserved the award for Services to the Feline Community after rescuing a cat from the Refrigerator Section of Lidl.

Instead our Doris woke up with intentions to get straight on with her deep clean.

I woke up to the sound of our Doris's earth-shattering scream. It were worse than a banshee cry, than when you accidentally step on the foot of a dachshund.

I staggered down the stairs to find her sprawled on the lino in the kitchen. The Speedclean three-thousand-and-six between her legs that did not have enough elasticity to be in the position they were in and she yelled at me, lord did she yell, she said, 'Get that ambulance on the phone, our 'arold, tell them as I've been the victim of foreign cleaning products, I'll write to my MP. Heads will roll, our 'arold, Switzerland won't know what's hit them.'

The ambulance were there within ten minutes. If heads were going to roll our Doris wouldn't stop with the Swiss.

I sat in the hospital waiting room whilst our Doris heckled at doctors in one of the consultation rooms. I could hear her scream, she said, 'Of course it's a ten, I've never dislocated my hip before in my life – is there another numeral you were looking for? Did you wish to delegate my pain to a number four so that you could save on morphine and increase your pay package? Because I won't stand for it, Doctor, I have paid my taxes I am due that morphine and if I'm not on a drip within three minutes I will write to the Partridge Mews Gazette informing them of your refusal to treat, in an adequate manner, a seventy-two year old woman who has lived in this town her entire life.' She's had a bad opinion of the NHS ever since she went to the vending machine for a Coca Cola and discovered they only had Dr Pepper Zero, a beverage she says is a deterrent for the morbidly obese that need never be created had anyone over eleven stone had some self-control.

I brought our Doris a sandwich from the café across the road and went to see her in her cubicle. She were sat on the bed reading her notes, her glasses balanced on the tip of her nose like some magician with a spoon, and she said to me, without even looking up she said, 'You ought to go home and check on the garden – it took an awful lot of planning to achieve the fifth house and I'm not prepared to throw it all away for a simple dislocated hip.'

I put the sandwich down, I were flabbergasted, I looked at her and I said to her, being too honest for my own good, I said, 'This garden safari will be the death of you, our Doris. In the last year you've caused more friction within the family than in the last fifty years, you've lost a tooth, you stopped me seeing my friends, you attacked someone and were almost imprisoned – you have been sentenced to community service and all because of this blasted garden safari. Look at Violet Grey, she had to leave town, and the way you're going you'll soon be following her example.'

Our Doris closed the brown folder all diplomatically as though she were about to announce a war and she said to me, emphasising the h, she said, 'Harold, in the last fifty years I have been through a lot and yet I have never lost my determination to better myself. I have never been one for horticulture, as well you know, yet I have always been accustomed to seeing a beautiful festoon of floristry displays in our back garden – all accomplished by you, my husband. Did it never occur to you that I wanted to share my husband's talents with the world?'

I must admit I were floundering. I said to her, I

said, 'You did this for me?'

She gave me the Look and said to me, she said, 'Of course I did it for you – I've always known you were worth fifth house in the garden safari, you work harder than most of the so-called gardeners in town. You can tell a hyacinth from a hibiscus. There isn't that long until the garden safari so please go home and get to work.'

I took a final look at our Doris, the world thundering in my head like a train through a tunnel and I left.

After I picked our Theo up from school, I took him home. I said to him, I said, 'Do you think I'm too harsh on your grandmother?'

He switched on the television and said to me, he said, 'What happened at the hospital?' I told him and he looked mildly stupefied before rising from his seat and heading towards the kitchen. 'I'll make a brew,' he said.

I followed him and said, 'You didn't answer my question.'

'Because there's no answer – you've been married to her for the majority of your life, you know one another more than anyone else, you can't expect your fourteen year old grandson to have an answer when he can't even figure out the value of x.' He added an extra sugar to my brew before handing it over.

'She told me that the garden safari is for me.'

'That's no surprise. For years she's been Mrs Doris Copeland and you've been her husband, she wanted to let you know that she notices you.'

'You seem to understand your grandmother more than I do.'

'I'm on the outside, it's easier to judge. Shall we have a look at the garden?' He opened the back door and looked out at the orchids and daffodils and assorted shrubberies. There were a light breeze and pollen in the air and all I could think about was how our Doris wasn't there to enjoy it.

I said to our Theo, I said, 'I don't think there's anything we need to do, Theo, it's been good enough for fifth house for over half a century, it'll be all right now.'

The paramedics brought our Doris home the next day, deposited her in the lounge and said no to the offer of a brew after a stern glare from the good wife herself. Once they'd gone I said to her, I said, 'How are you feeling?'

And she said, 'We've got a lot to do, our 'arold.'

'I know,' I said.

Over the next fortnight the WI spent more time at our house – we went through that many tea bags shares in PG Tips must've gone through the roof. Pandra O'Malley bought some hanging baskets from Mrs Singh's that found their way to the front door as our Doris thought that they might take away from the passionate nuances of our themed back garden. I said to her, I said, 'I never made any theme to the garden, our Doris.'

The wheelchair gave her even more of a threat of menace as she said to me, she said, 'That's because there isn't one, our 'arold. Anyone who asks will question the theme and I will merely state that you've always been a fan of Jackson Pollock.'

I'd never seen any of Jackson Pollock's work before in my life but Theo showed me a few images on Google that meant I'd be okay to give the vague impression I actually knew a thing or two about art that didn't come from the few night classes I'd taken.

On the eve of the garden safari I helped our Doris pick out her clothes – she'd chosen her Dorothy Perkins floral print dress and coral blue sandals with a light cream scarf. For me, she chose navy blue trousers and a white shirt; it's easier to dress a man, especially one whose wife keeps sending his clothes to Sue Ryder.

Our Angela arrived early the next morning to help our Doris get dressed and I went to make sure the path was clean, swept leaves away from the drive, set up Alf on the drive to make sure all dog walkers cleaned up their mess.

The first visitors arrived at about eleven o'clock. They'd already been to Peter Thomson's first house, a feat we were told was not as advertised as he had headed off to Birmingham to visit his former sister-in-law, leaving nothing more than a note on his front door, scrawled in wax crayon. Pandra O'Malley and her new boyfriend commented on the hanging baskets and how they were the perfect introduction to our garden and that Mrs Glover of the third house had hanging baskets but they were filled with aphids and had thus been surrounded by black bin liners – making the garden more of a wake than a safari.

Our Doris placed herself at the front door beside a table of refreshments, and assembled the guests. She were ever the diplomat asking after people's children and grandchildren – introducing them to our themed garden.

Mrs Sterling drew particular attention to our Doris's salmon blinis saying as they were the perfect texture and that light they practically melted on her tongue. Her husband looked a bit disgruntled but that's to be expected from Arthur Sterling, a man whose father spent the majority of his final years upset he hadn't died fighting for his country – he got an infected case of impetigo that finally saw him off.

Theo was the perfect gentleman. He wooed the grandmother's paying particular attention to Opal Montague's dress, she's worn the same dress to all festive occasions since nineteen-eighty-five but no one says anything because her father was found in a ditch with Michael Preston.

Everything was going fine until she appeared, like a spectre of death; Janice Dooley of Little Street. She wore a violet dress our Doris wouldn't approve of that emphasised her varicose veins perfectly. It clung to each and every curve of her body, as though it had been made especially to show off her cellulite.

I headed straight towards her but it was our Doris who intercepted her. Our Angela must've got a head start with wheeling her over. She sat with a cup of tea on her lap which she handed to Janice – the entire party froze, I felt like we were in a Western and a tumbleweed would be there any moment. Our Doris said to her, she said, 'I am glad you have taken it upon yourself to join us on this day, Ms Dooley, in celebration of the people of Partridge Mews. Please do take a moment to enjoy the horticultural display my husband so lovingly created. Let us put our differences aside on today of all days.'

'Mrs Copeland, I only came to see what all the fuss was about. After all, the majority of us here know that you've never lifted a finger in your life.'

And I don't know where it came from, I've never felt the need to defend my wife before, she's perfectly good enough at it herself, I said to her, I said, 'Why don't you just beggar off, Janice? You have spent your life making a mockery of all of us – you're lucky our

Doris stopped beating you in the graveyard because if it had been me, I wouldn't have stopped until you were returned to the primordial ooze you escaped from.'

The cup of tea were bundled back in our Doris's hands as Janice said to me, she said, 'I'm glad that you are able to have faith in your wife, Mr Copeland, because so many people are unable to.'

'I think it would be best if you shut your mouth and just left because frankly not a single person here would care to hear what you have to say.' And with that, Janice Dooley of Little Street left Shakespeare Avenue and the fifth house of the garden safari. Our Doris didn't say anything but there were a definite glimmer of something in her eyes.

As the day wore on and the food decreased and folk went home, me and our Doris were left alone together. I sat in my deck chair next to her in her wheelchair and we stared out at the garden, inhaling the pollen, the falling sun warm against our faces and our Doris took one look at me and said to me, she said 'I think you should have an affair.'

Now I were the one giving her The Look. I wondered if this were a sign of a stroke. I focused on her face, her lips weren't drooping – no more than usual anyway. At seventy-two years old you've got to expect some sagging. I must've been looking a bit funny because she whacked her arm against my stomach.

'What's all that about? Looking at me like I've flipped my lid. I think you should have an affair.'

I said to her, I said, 'Doris, we have been married for fifty four years, why do you want me to run into the arms of some other poor so-and-so?'

That got her, I could tell because she stared up at the big tree in the garden, held her hands together and said nothing. Her eyes were all glazed over. She were thinking. If I've learnt anything these past few decades it's not to interrupt her when she's thinking.

Then she sighed and said, 'I'd like to get my ironing done.'

I said to her, 'You can iron – I'll take thee inside right now and you can iron. I don't need to have an affair.'

She said, 'You get under my feet.'

I said, 'Oh.'

Usually right about now, we'd be sat in the lounge watching Granada Reports. I should have brought a Thermos. A cup of sweet tea is what she needed. That'd stop her thinking about affairs. I'm seventy four, I don't have the sense to run off with a younger woman. Even with permission, I think our Doris would kill me – and worse, she'd probably enjoy it.

She looked at me and said, 'I'd like a brew and a custard cream.'

I said, 'Shall we go inside?'

That got me The Look. 'Well where else will we bleeding go? Pontefract?'

I started to wheel her indoors and I said to her, it must have been the feeling of the day, the sun was shining as it began it's early evening descent and I said 'I love you, you know, our Doris?'

I saw something similar to a smile on her face and she said to me, she said, 'After fifty four years I should bleeding well think so.' And she held my hand as a lone slug trailed its way towards the chrysanthemums.

Acknowledgements

All writers have help when creating a book and Our Doris has had much assistance in making her way into the world.

First, thank you to Lindsey for her friendship, guidance, support, and listening to all of the rambles and rants over the years. You have gone above and beyond and the fact that you proof-read Our Doris is something I will be forever grateful for.

The book would not have seen the light of day if it hadn't been for the Macclesfield Creative Writing Group. Especial thanks is due to Margaret Holbrook who has answered my countless emails, critiqued drafts and helped me realise that Doris deserved a book of her own. If you hadn't been there I wouldn't have had all the opportunities I have and I thank you for that.

Thanks are also due to Abercrombie, Joy Winkler, Jill Walsh, Cathryn Heathcote, Karen Ross, Sandy Milsom and Phil Poyser for encouragement, conversations and the general reminder that I had a book to write.

Thank you to the readers, audience members and librarians for their support in helping Our Doris reach the masses.

For those of you who have been around since the beginning, until next time, that is all.

Below is the first short monologue I wrote that inspired Our Doris. Included in the Macclesfield Creative Writing Group's first anthology and performed to a few audiences it is only fitting that it should be featured here, as without this tale there would be no book.

BREAD

Our Doris wants me to buy some bread but it's getting too much hassle nowadays. There's bread for fat people, bread for folk who don't care and bread for vegans – which I imagine tastes like cardboard. When Vanessa Feltz started on about carrot juice everyone was on it – then she got fat again and we've not bothered since. I hear she had her stomach choked – had some sort of band shoved down there and hoped for the best. I say, the best way to cure that thing would've been to padlock the fridge door.

I said to our Doris, I said, 'Why be a vegan? You won't have much fun.' She turned to me and said, 'If I wish to stop consuming animal produce, our 'arold I will. Eating meat is murder! And don't you forget it. Honestly – it's just too stressful to think about.' She took a bite of her bacon sandwich and started harping on about how Marcia at No. 47 was a vegan, and had offered to induct her. I said, 'What do you mean, "induct"? What do you do, dance around a maypole whilst burning a sacrificial stick of celery?' She rolled her eyes at this and told me it was a complex diet that with proper practice could be extremely fulfilling. She'd quit after a week – she said they wanted her shoes because they were leather – she said they were Clarks and that was the end of that matter entirely.

But doing this everyday gets me down. I stand till me legs are sore for the paper boy – our Doris doesn't trust him because his grandfather's from Cheadle and she doesn't want to be associated with them folk, thank-you-very-much. I could be in bed, not that our Doris notices anymore. She hit ... well that age and gave up sexual endeavours for Maeve Binchy – who she now says is getting very racy. If a woman wrapping a cardigan around herself is racy, what are her thoughts on S&M? Clipping yourself with the razor? We were never into strange stuff, I've never had a fetish. I thought it would come with age, but now Ann Widdecombe's looking attractive, so I guess I waited too long. Our Doris did consider swinging for a time, until she found out it didn't involve line dancing.

So the paper boy's grandfather's from Cheadle and not to be trusted – same as the paper boy. And I've got to decide on a loaf of bread. Our Doris wants Granary, but I could do without bird seed in me dentures for the next week. I like white bread; it's everything British: stodgy, and if taken the wrong way can cause heart attack. It's not like Muesli – sultanas and nuts and weird flaky things; I've seen more nutritious tat in rabbit muck.

We had a rabbit once: Doris's idea. It was white with red eyes – she called it Snowy and I didn't bother. It'd only eat steak; stupid, carnivorous beggar – I dunno why she didn't knock it on the head. We didn't kill it in the end, it had heart attack – that didn't kill it. I tripped over on the way to the vet's and it got run over by a Tesco lorry. I suppose every little does help. I told our Doris the vet put it down, more humane that way – he's still on the Christmas card list, so I suppose she didn't mind.

You can get best of both bread now, can't you? Maybe she'd enjoy a white loaf that keeps her regular. Although I don't know whether she could cope with multi-cultural bread, she struggled when we went to Guernsey. We weren't there for long when she decided she hadn't dipped her nets and we had to come back because she couldn't have Lillian from down the street, thinking that she was a bad housewife. I bet she still wants seeds in the bread, whatever the race. If she does, I'll nip into the pet shop and get em cheap, no point throwing money away, just for a bit of bird seed.

I'm going inside for a brew – the paper boy can wait – I'm not catching pneumonia for a glance at The Times.